ADVANCE PRAISE FOR THE BOOK

Chitranshul Sinha's trenchant exposition of the history of the sedition law in India makes an exceptionally well-researched and strongly argued case against this antiquated and undemocratic tool of repression. His exceptionally readable analysis has been critically positioned within the structures and practices through which the concept of sedition emerged, making it an insightful work of great relevance for our times'—Shashi Tharoor, member of Parliament from Thiruvananthapuram

The book concisely chronicles the entire 150-year journey of the law of sedition from its insertion in the Indian Penal Code in 1870. Despite the extensive and inevitable legal content, the book is highly readable and Chitranshul Sinha makes a compelling case for the repeal of Section 124A—as has been done in the UK, the country of its origin'—Arvind P. Datar, Senior Advocate

THE
GREAT
REPRESSION

THE

GREAT

REPRESSION

THE STORY OF
SEDITION IN INDIA

CHITRANSHUL SINHA

PENGUIN
VIKING
An imprint of Penguin Random House

VIKING

USA | Canada | UK | Ireland | Australia
New Zealand | India | South Africa | China

Viking is part of the Penguin Random House group of companies
whose addresses can be found at global.penguinrandomhouse.com

Published by Penguin Random House India Pvt. Ltd
7th Floor, Infinity Tower C, DLF Cyber City,
Gurgaon 122 002, Haryana, India

First published in Viking by Penguin Random House India 2019

Copyright © Chitranshul Sinha 2019

10 9 8 7 6 5 4 3 2 1

The views and opinions expressed in this book are the author's own and the
facts are as reported by him which have been verified to the extent possible, and
the publishers are not in any way liable for the same.

ISBN 9780670091133

Typeset in Sabon by Manipal Digital Systems, Manipal
Printed at Replika Press Pvt. Ltd, India

www.penguin.co.in

*To the innumerable nameless seditionists
to whom we owe our freedom and our republic*

'*The Constitution fails when a cartoonist is jailed for sedition.*'

Justice Dhananjaya Y. Chandrachud

Contents

PART III: SEDITION IN THE REPUBLIC

Acknowledgements

The idea of writing a book, any book, took flight when Rukun Kaul, a dear friend, declared one fine evening that she thought I was going to write a book. This decree was pronounced while discussing the future and our expectations from it. She followed up her pronouncement by connecting me to Manasi Subramaniam, editor extraordinaire at Penguin Random House India. Manasi then guided me towards the idea of writing the story of sedition in India and helped me crystallize the pitch and the structure. After that she granted me complete freedom and never ever interfered or tried to influence my work. As a professional working in a high-stress environment, being granted such freedom was a breath of fresh air. Thank you, Rukun, and thank you, Manasi.

The idea of writing anything for public consumption was given a push by another dear friend, Apar Gupta. He pushed me to write and connected me with Rukmini Srinivasan at Huffington Post, for whom I wrote my first article. Rituparna Chatterjee, who was then an editor at Huffington Post, and whom I have the privilege to call a friend now, enabled me to write even more and helped me develop my writing style as well as my confidence. Thanks, guys.

The amount of research involved in this book was monumental. I would not have been able to take a deep dive without the help of my colleague Sonali Khanna, who is a bright young lawyer to watch out for, and Akshay Sharma, who is one of the brightest law students I have come across. Deepa Kumar helped me source research material which otherwise would have been unobtainable for me thanks to the gatekeepers of knowledge. I also want to thank all my colleagues in my office for their support and constant encouragement. Dua Associates, the law firm where I work, has one of the best work environments which granted me the freedom to write while working full-time.

I owe a debt of gratitude to my friends and colleagues Alok P. Kumar, Gautam Bhatia, Aastha Dhaon and Konark Tyagi for looking at my manuscript despite having extremely busy lives. Their suggestions and inputs were invaluable and helped me provide the final shape to this book. Siddharth Singh chipped in with excellent tips and advice despite being occupied with writing his own book, the excellent *The Great Smog of India*. Asmita Bakshi and Avantika Mehta, excellent journalists both, provided brilliant suggestions for deciding the book's title, which is an extremely underrated task. Super-cop A. Sai Manohar (IPS) provided insights and guidance on legal procedure and data without which a critical part of the book would have remained insufficient. His grace was demonstrated by the fact that he took time out to help me despite being busy beyond belief. I am really grateful for his help. Special thanks to my brother, Ayushman, for being my sounding board and for patiently listening to my rants.

This book would never have been completed without the support of Esha Sharma, my wife, who suffered through a year of lost weekends (and weekdays) with nothing but encouragement. She forsook important occasions for my sake, raised my spirits and kept me on the right path every time I was just about ready to throw in the towel. Her help at crucial junctures is invaluable. This book is as much hers, if not more, as it is mine.

Lastly, writing in this medium would not have been possible without the English language education that my parents provided me with despite all odds. They ensured that my brother and I studied in the best schools and colleges while fighting off financial constraints. My brother and I never felt that we did not have enough, or we were not good enough. They taught us life.

Prologue

The *Indian Express* published a story on 20 June 2018 about how the police in the Rohtas district of Bihar arrested eight people, five of whom were minors, on charges of sedition for dancing to a song whose lyrics meant, 'We are Pakistani mujahids, protectors of Earth; if you challenge us even by mistake, we will cut you up.' The arrests occurred after a video of the song and dance was given to the police by a right-wing organization.

'They must have danced to the beat—the song barely played for three or four minutes,' the parent of one of the boys said. According to the brother of another minor boy, 'The children were dancing in joy. Most of them realized that some objectionable and controversial song had been played only after the ruckus following police intervention.' The father of another boy said, 'Sedition charges against these little boys have hurt us badly. There has never been any communal riot in Nasriganj's history. In this town you can still hear the azaan and Ram *dhun* going on simultaneously. We are trying to hire a good lawyer and pinning all hopes on the judiciary.'

The Indian Penal Code (IPC) of 1860 was the first ever codification of offences and penalties in India. Chapter VI of the Indian Penal Code provides for 'Of Offences against the State', within which falls Section 124A which lays down the offence of 'sedition'. The capital alphabet 'A' suffixed to 124 signifies that the provision was not a part of the original penal code as enacted in 1860. Section 124A was slipped in between Section 124 ('assaulting President, Governor, etc. with intent to compel or restrain the exercise of any lawful power') and Section 125 ('waging war against any Asiatic power in alliance with the Government of India') of the code in the year 1870, marking the first time that sedition was defined in a statute in the common law system.

Section 124A was amended for the first time in 1898, and thereafter underwent multiple changes in the years 1937, 1948, 1950, 1951 and 1955. After the amendment of 1955, Section 124A has been left untouched by Parliament, and in its present form reads as under:

> Sedition.—Whoever, by words, either spoken or written, or by signs, or by visible representation, or otherwise, brings or attempts to bring into hatred or contempt, or excites or attempts to excite disaffection towards, the Government established by law in India, shall be punished with imprisonment for life, to which fine may be added, or with imprisonment which may extend to three years, to which fine may be added, or with fine.
>
> Explanation 1.—The expression 'disaffection' includes disloyalty and all feelings of enmity.
>
> Explanation 2.—Comments expressing disapprobation of the measures of the Government with a view to obtain their alteration by lawful

means, without exciting or attempting to excite hatred, contempt or disaffection, do not constitute an offence under this section.

Explanation 3.—Comments expressing disapprobation of the administrative or other action of the Government without exciting or attempting to excite hatred, contempt or disaffection, do not constitute an offence under this section.

The first annual report on 'Crime in India' was published for the year 1953 by the Intelligence Bureau which introduced a uniform system of maintaining crime statistics throughout the country. The report covered only the major heads of crimes, being murder, dacoity, robbery, kidnapping, housebreaking and theft. The entire report along with appendices was twenty-one pages long. Thereafter, the annual report has been published for all years till 2016, barring 1962, which was the year of the Indo-China war.

The National Crime Records Bureau (NCRB) is the agency now responsible for the collection of statistics and publication of the report, which has grown in volume and now features an expanded categorization of offences. However, offences against the State did not find a separate mention for sixty years. The report created a separate category for offences against the State in the year 2014 for the first time. In its introduction to the chapter on offences against the State, it says:

Broadly speaking, all crimes are against the state, or government, insofar as it disturbs the public order. But there are some criminal activities that are directed against the existence of the state itself viz. treason, sedition, and rebellion. Treason is the crime of betraying a nation by acts considered dangerous to its security like selling military secrets to a foreign power, giving aid to the enemy in time of war etc. Sedition refers generally to the offence related to conduct or speech inciting people to rebel against the authority of a state or government. Rebellion is the attempted overthrow of a government; if it succeeds it is a coup, or revolution.

A total of forty-seven cases of sedition under Section 124A of the IPC were reported for the year 2014 for which a total of fifty-eight people were arrested. This number fell to thirty cases in 2015 with seventy-three people arrested, but rose to thirty-five in 2016 with forty-eight arrests. At the end of 2016, out of all the pending cases, sixty-one cases under Section 124A were still pending investigation by the police. The charge-sheeting rate for cases of sedition stood at 66.7 per cent, which implies that over 33 per cent cases where an offence of sedition was alleged did not even reach trial and were closed by the police. In fact, out of the forty-eight people arrested for sedition in 2016, only twenty-six people were charge-sheeted.

The year 2016 saw thirty-four trials for sedition, out of which only three cases were concluded, resulting in a single conviction and two acquittals according to the report. Thus, at the end of 2016, thirty-one trials were still pending adjudication.

The recorded data demonstrates that out of all the recorded cases there has been just a single conviction. The NCRB data records that the conviction was in the mineral-rich eastern state of Jharkhand, which incidentally also recorded the highest number of cases under Section 124A. Note that there is a raging internal conflict in the state with Maoist insurgents, with the government locked in a bitter battle with them for the past many years, which shows no signs of concluding any time soon. Most recently, cases for sedition have been lodged against student leaders, journalists and even people supporting Pakistan in a match against India. Historically, Section 124A has been used to muzzle voices against the establishment, be it journalists or activists.

In 2016, Common Cause, an NGO, filed a writ petition against the Union of India before the Supreme Court of India asking for guidelines to be laid down for registration of cases under Section 124A. The writ petition asked that police authorities and magistrates be directed to provide a reasoned order certifying that the 'seditious act' either led to the incitement of violence or had the tendency or the intention to create public disorder before any FIR was filed or any arrest made or investigation directed on the charges of sedition against any individual. The Supreme Court, however, did not deem it necessary to issue such specific directions, but by its order on 5 September 2016 directed that authorities must be mindful of the 1962 Constitution Bench judgment of the Supreme Court in *Kedar Nath Singh v. State of Bihar*.

Five judges of the Supreme Court led by then Chief Justice of India Bhuvaneshwar Prasad Sinha unanimously held in the *Kedar Nath* case that:

It is well settled that if certain provisions of law construed in one way would make them consistent with the Constitution, and another interpretation would render them unconstitutional, the Court would lean in favour of the former construction. The provisions of the sections read as a whole, along with the explanations, make it reasonably clear that the sections aim at rendering penal only such activities as would be intended, or have a tendency, to create disorder or disturbance of public peace by resort to violence. As already pointed out, the explanations appended to the main body of the section make it clear that criticism of public measures or comment on Government action, however strongly worded, would be within reasonable limits and would be consistent with the fundamental right of freedom of speech and expression. It is only when the words, written or spoken, etc. which have the pernicious tendency or intention of creating public disorder or disturbance of law and order that the law steps in to prevent such activities in the interest of public order. So construed, the section, in our opinion, strikes the correct balance between individual fundamental rights and the interest of public order. It is also well settled that in interpreting an enactment the Court should have regard not merely to the literal meaning of the words used, but also take into consideration the antecedent history of the legislation, its purpose and the mischief it seeks to suppress.

Therefore, in simple words, a precondition for conviction under Section 124A would be that the alleged seditious act should either be violent or lead to, or attempt to lead to, violent acts.

India is arguably considered one of the most mature parliamentary democracies in the world, apart from being the largest. Freedom of speech and expression, freedom to peacefully protest and freedom of political activism are essential for mature democracies as diverse as ours. The diversity and population of this country entails conflicting views and opposition to the establishment. The law against sedition may appear out of place in such a society, and the reasons for its existence can only be understood with a look at the history of evolution of the legal and judicial system in India, and the origin and philosophy of criminal law in India. More importantly, the law against sedition must be understood from the history of its application and implementation.

This book will attempt to tell the story of sedition, and the reasons and desirability of its continued existence.

PART I

ORIGIN STORY

1

Company Raj: Seeds of the Modern Indian Legal System

Vasco da Gama, a Portuguese explorer, discovered a sea route to India around the Cape of Good Hope in Africa in 1498 and landed in Calicut in what is now Kerala. This important discovery of an all-sea route opened the doors to Asia for Western European nations which had been hampered in their trade with the East due to a monopoly of the Mediterranean States, and later by the Turks as they controlled land access to Asia. The fifteenth century saw the growth of Portugal and Spain into naval powers which enabled the dispatching of sovereign-backed explorers to discover sea-based trade routes to Asia and the West. These adventures culminated in the discovery of a sea passage to India and other Asian regions.

The beginning of the seventeenth century saw the birth of the two most powerful trading corporations which would go on to dominate trade with Asia for a long time. In England, an association of merchants and traders known as Merchant Adventurers was formed in 1599. Better known as the East India Company, the association was granted a charter by Queen Elizabeth on 31 December 1600 with the exclusive privilege and right to trade with the 'East Indies'. This was followed by the incorporation of the Dutch East India Company under a parliamentary charter in 1602 with the same purpose of trade in Asian spices, mainly with South East Asia, India, Malay and Sri Lanka.[1] The East India Company received another commission by King James I in 1609, making its charter perpetual in 1609, subject to termination with three years' notice.[2]

In 1613, the Company established its first Indian factory—essentially a trading post—in Surat with the permission of the Mughal Emperor Jehangir,[3] who subsequently permitted the Company to establish factories at various places along the west coast. Surat was chosen by the Company on the basis of its importance as a port which saw a lot of traffic, especially for Muslim travellers who sailed to the holy lands, and for trade with Arab countries.[4] Interestingly, India was not the main focus of the East India Company whose main target market was South East Asia and Malay, where it was competing with the Dutch. However, the Dutch repelled attempts by the English to establish control over trade with South East Asia, which resulted in the English East India Company being consigned to focus its efforts on the Indian subcontinent.[5]

John William Kaye says, 'From the Bombay Coast, where the Company factors first settled themselves, they made their way by land to Agra, then rounded Cape Cormorin,[6] settled themselves on the Coast of Madras, and soon stretched up the Bay of Bengal, to establish themselves in that rich province.' The Company employed a system where their ships would sail from India with cargo, leaving behind agents known as 'factors' who would negotiate with local traders for the sale of cargo brought from England and for the purchase of goods to be sent back on the Company's ships. English employees of the Company located in its factories in India were subject to two different systems of law. In their relations with the natives, and any disputes with them or offences against them, the English were subject to the laws which governed the natives, and the disputes or offences were adjudicated by the local system of dispensation of justice. However, when it came to maintaining discipline on the vessels of the Company, or in cases of offences by an English subject employed by the Company against another such subject, martial law was employed to adjudicate and impose punishments.[7]

In this regard, the Company received a royal grant from the British Crown on 14 December 1615 authorizing it to issue commissions providing for adjudication on offences and imposition of punishments on its subjects under martial law. The only condition imposed by the grant was that any case which could lead to a death penalty had to be tried before a jury.[8] This grant enabled the Company to issue commissions without needing to approach the king for each voyage, as was the practice earlier. However, this grant was limited to offences committed on voyages.

The earliest recorded criminal trial pursuant to the royal grant of 1615 involved a Company employee named Gregory Lellington in Surat.[9] He was accused of murdering an Englishman by the name of Henry Barton, an employee sailing on board the *James,* a ship belonging to the Company, on 16 February 1616. He was charged with the crime on 28 February 1616 and his trial was held on a ship named *Charles* off the coast of Surat. Lellington confessed to killing Barton and was duly sentenced to death by Henry Pepwell (chief commander of the fleet) and Thomas Kerridge (chief of the factory). Lellington, someone with an actual death wish, desired an immediate execution. The executioners were happy to oblige and shot him the very next day to end his misery.[10]

On land, however, there existed a situation where the employees of the Company were at the mercy of local laws and judicial systems when it came to their disputes with the native population. The native rulers did not really bother about disputes between Englishmen. This necessitated another royal grant of 1623 which extended the grant of 1615 for jurisdiction over offences *inter se* the servants of the Company located in India. This grant was again subject to the same condition as earlier, that is, offences punishable by death were to be tried before a jury.[11] Mutiny, murder and any other felonies were offences punishable by death which required a jury trial. The power to adjudicate under the grant was placed with the president or chief of the factory, thereby empowering the Company to enforce the rule of law on high seas as well as land.[12] By 1623,[13] the Company had also established factories at Ahmedabad, Broach,[14] Agra and Masulipatnam.[15]

However, the royal grant of 1623 did not specify the territory over which the grant had been made but only provided for imposition of martial law. This necessitated another grant in 1624 which empowered the Company to issue commissions to the presidents of factories in India to punish English employees of the Company under martial law as well as under English 'Common Law'. This empowerment was for trial of offences on land as well as on the high seas.[16]

The control of the East India Company and the operations of the Company in India vested with the court of directors of the Company, which exercised such control under instructions from the Crown, which in turn acted through a secretary of state.[17] This structure was overhauled only towards the end of the eighteenth century, but more on that later.

The East India Company, being an expansionary enterprise, had already set up a factory at Masulipatnam in

1611 in present-day Andhra Pradesh, and it went on to set up more trading posts over the course of the next couple of decades. In 1639, a place called Madraspatnam[18] drew the attention of the English due to the superior quality of cloth available for trade as compared to its other posts on the east coast. The Company obtained the lease of the locality from the local ruler, the *nayak*, and got permission to build fortifications. The fort was named Fort St George after the patron saint of England. Previously under the control of the Bantam Presidency located in Java, Fort St George was elevated to a presidency by the English in 1653, which was the birth of the Madras Presidency. The presidency was administered by a governor and a council of three. One of the governors of Madras was Elihu Yale, who served from 1687 to 1692, after whom Yale University in the USA is named. The Madras Presidency, after many conflicts with the French and native rulers, spread to almost all of present-day Tamil Nadu, present-day Andhra Pradesh and parts of present-day Karnataka (including the Malabar coast) by the end of the eighteenth century.[19]

On the west coast, the Company established the Bombay Presidency, which stretched from Sindh in the north, parts of present-day Gujarat till Daman, and down the Western Ghats up to Karwar in present-day Karnataka. The Presidency was administered from Surat before the control shifted to Bombay. The island of Bombay became a part of the English empire in 1665 once it was ceded by Portugal as part of the dowry for the marriage of Princess Catherine of Portugal to King Charles II of England.[20]

Digressing for a moment, the marriage of the two royals in 1662 was unique because it was carried out in proxy. The king was not present in Lisbon when the ceremony was conducted under Catholic customs. The crowds carried full-size portraits of the royal couple in a procession to celebrate the union. Only upon Catherine's arrival in England was the marriage formalized under Protestant customs in the presence of both bride and groom.[21]

The king transferred the control of the island of Bombay to the East India Company in 1668, and eventually in 1687 Bombay was elevated to the seat of the presidency which was earlier located at Surat. Bombay received this honour due to its defensible nature which was seen as an advantage by the Company and the English. The city of Bombay prospered and grew, along with the growth of the presidency.[22]

Up in the Gangetic plains, the Company had established its first factory in Bengal in 1640[23] at Hooghly, and was permitted to set up factories in Patna, Balasore, Dhaka, etc. in the 1650s. It only purchased land rights, called zamindari, of three villages in Bengal in 1698 from the Mughals. The site of the acquisition went on to become present-day Kolkata. It was made the headquarters of the East India Company in Bengal and was fortified as Fort William, named after King William III. After conflicts with the Mughals and the French, the English established their hold over Bengal in 1757 under the lame duck Nawab Mir Jafar, who had been placed in that position by the English, after defeating Siraj-ud-Daulah at the Battle of Plassey. Eventually, the British established complete control over Bengal, Bihar, Awadh and Orissa in 1765, thus establishing the prosperous Bengal Presidency with its seat at Calcutta—prosperous for the Company but ruinous for Bengal. Thus commenced the actual rise of the British political and military empire in India, and the East India Company started transforming from a trading corporation into a territorial and colonial force. The Company assumed *dewani* rights and thus controlled the civil justice system, but the *nizami* or criminal justice powers remained with the nizam and his administrators.[24]

The celebrated judgment of the Privy Council in *Ryots of Garabandho v. Zamindar of Parlakimedi*[25] sheds light on the justice system of the presidencies. The administration of law and the judicial system in India at this stage was dual in nature. Under the Mughal Empire, Hindus and Muslims were subject to their personal laws with regard to civil cases, but as far as criminal cases were concerned Mohammedan law was largely applied for deciding the punishment to be imposed. The judicial tribunals mostly comprised of native clerics overseen by the local rulers. The English exercised judicial power over their subjects in accordance with English law, but the same could not be applied to the natives. A civilian judicial system established by the English did exist in the three presidencies, but it largely concerned itself with disputes between its subjects and offences against the English. In places where it had to be exercised on the local populace, natives who were well versed in the personal laws of Hindus and Muslims were employed. There was absolutely no uniformity, mainly due to the diversity of the Indian populace and the different systems of administration in the three presidencies. The first change came about in 1773 when the British Parliament established a Supreme Court in Calcutta to replace the existing system which exercised jurisdiction over the Company's employees and inhabitants of its towns and factories in Bengal and Bihar. This was a part of the British Parliament's first attempt to take control of the administration of the Company.

Prior to the Company taking over, the dispensation of criminal justice was left to the native administrators or zamindars who passed sentences according to their whims and even handed out death sentences. In 1790, the Company started taking control of the criminal justice system against natives using Mohammedan penal laws for both Muslims and Hindus, with certain adjustments made whenever the defendant was a Hindu. Appeals from civil and criminal cases went to the Sadar Dewani Adalat and Sadar Nizami Adalat. However, none of the courts established by the Company had any jurisdiction over British subjects who were not servants of the Company. In fact, the Company did not permit any British subject to reside beyond ten miles from the capital unless they voluntarily submitted to the jurisdiction of such district courts outside the ten-mile limit.

Parallelly, the Supreme Court at this time was tasked by the British Parliament with jurisdiction over British subjects residing in the towns and settlements within the presidency, and subject to the protection of the Company. The Supreme Court applied English laws to exercise such jurisdiction and decided upon civil and criminal complaints against both English and Indian servants of the Company. Such sweeping powers of the Supreme Court were restricted in 1781 by excluding revenue matters and official actions of the principal officer of the Company from its jurisdiction. Further, the Supreme Court was mandated to apply Hindu and Mohammedan law against Indian defendants in accordance with their religion. The above system was extended to the Madras and Bombay presidencies in the first decade of the nineteenth century. The powers of the Supreme Court were curbed due to active lobbying by the Company led by Warren Hastings, the governor general of Bengal.

Earlier in 1780, conflict between the Supreme Court's and the Company's system of administration reached a head during the famous case of Raja Sundernarain, who was the zamindar of Cosijurrah (which lies in present-day Midnapore in Bengal). Kashinath, a resident of Calcutta, had lent money to the raja, who defaulted in its payment, which led to Kashinath filing a suit against him in the Supreme Court. The Supreme Court issued a warrant against the raja by holding that he was a servant of the Company as he collected revenue on its behalf. While the raja avoided the warrant, the Council of the Governor General of Bengal issued instructions to all zamindars that they could ignore the orders of the Supreme Court as they did not fall under its jurisdiction because of being natives. Thereafter, the Supreme Court sent a sheriff to enforce its warrant and to establish its authority over the zamindars. The Company saw this as an affront to their authority and sent armed forces to repel the sheriff. By doing so, the Company undermined the Supreme Court and reasserted its authority over revenue and civil matters in the presidency. It is said that the Cosijurrah case was the lowest point between the Company and the Supreme Court which culminated in restrictions on the jurisdiction and powers of the Supreme Court.[26]

All this while, the British Parliament was actively making efforts to exercise greater control over the East India Company as it realized that the Company was not a mere trading corporation any more. It had attained the characteristics of an imperial power and was slowly turning into a monster with a mind of its own. Unfair trade practices and extortionate revenue collection by the Company resulted in massive economic crises for the natives. Hoarding and export of food grain to the disadvantage of local agriculturists and consumers and no attention to the economic plight of the natives culminated in the first Great Bengal Famine which occurred between 1769 to 1773, causing the deaths of about 10 million people, or one-third of the population of Bengal, Bihar and Orissa. The British Parliament was conscious of the atrocities and unregulated commercial conduct of the

Company which was causing resentment amongst the natives in India.

In 1784, the Parliament, by way of an Act,[27] placed the control of the Company under a Board of Commissioners to control the affairs of India, called the Board of Control. Its members were the chancellor of the exchequer, a secretary of state and four privy councillors appointed by the Crown. The Board was in charge of the military and political activities of the Company.[28]

Having said that, it would be amiss to not point out that the British government enjoyed a level of control over the political and military affairs of the East India Company in India, albeit unofficially, even prior to 1784. Not a very well-known fact, but there existed a glamorously named Secret Committee which comprised a small number of directors of the Company who were responsible for the relay of political and military instructions from the British cabinet from time to time. This covert communication system was formalized by Pitt's Act of 1784, and the Secret Committee became an official conduit for instructions and information between the Board of Control and administrators of the Indian presidencies. The Secret Committee went on to play a major role in the expansion of the Company's—and by proxy Britain's—political control in India.[29]

One must ask the question: What was the need for the British to introduce a structured legal system and bring uniformity of justice dispensation for the natives? They could have simply applied English law over the British subjects and non-native servants of the Company, or even all servants of the Company, native or otherwise. At the end of the day, the Company was a for-profit corporation and not a vehicle for social reform or change. So, the question arises, where was the need for replacing or modifying indigenous law for justice delivery?

The answer to this lies in the principle of free markets. The Hindus were governed by laws of the Shastras[30] and customary laws. Such customs recognized a caste system which created a feudal structure consisting of brahmins, kshatriyas, vaish and shudras (priests/intellectuals, warriors, traders and untouchables) in that order of importance. This structure ensured there was no equality of status which, according to the British, acted as a hurdle for a free market.[31] The Company could only profit if indigenous society enabled free commerce, and so it went about trying to change the same. It woefully failed to disturb the caste system, an evil which prevails till date, but it succeeded in transforming the law and the judicial system. According to Galanter,[32] the British made an attempt to compile Hindu laws but were hindered by the fact that there was no uniformity in the application of customary law, and even the Shastras were not entirely helpful. Muslim laws were used for criminal cases, with regulations making modifications for its applicability to Hindus. However, the driving principle behind the application of the laws, by virtue of the adjudicators being British, were the principles of justice, equity and good conscience. Another change which was brought forth was the introduction of formal systems of appeal, rules of procedure, and the creation of a class of professionals to plead and argue before the Courts. On this, Galanter quotes Maine:[33]

At the touch of a Judge of the Supreme Court, who had been trained in the English school of special pleading, and had probably come to the East in the maturity of life, the rule of natural law dissolved and, with or without his intention, was to a great extent replaced by rules having their origin in English law-books. Under the hands of the judges of the Sudder

Courts, who had lived since their boyhood among the people of the Country, the native rules hardened and contracted a rigidity which they never had in real native practice.

These changes filled the gaps created by the lack of uniformity in law and forever changed how justice was dispensed in India.

2

Bentham, Mill and Macaulay

Nanda Kumar[1] was an upper-caste Hindu in the employ of the nawab of Bengal. He rose through the ranks to become the dewan of Hooghly in 1752 and went on to become the military governor of Hooghly. Hooghly was the first European settlement in Bengal, having been established as a trading centre by the Portuguese who were eventually driven out by Shah Jahan. Hooghly was a district of importance for trade and was the principal trading centre for the British before Calcutta. Nanda Kumar became extremely powerful and was bestowed with the title of 'maharaja' by the Mughal nawab. His prominence and power did not go down well with Warren Hastings, who was a high-ranking Company official at Murshidabad before being elevated to the governorship of Bengal in 1772. Hastings and Nanda Kumar resented each other for various reasons, and Hastings thought of Nanda Kumar as deceitful and cunning.

Their mutual hatred culminated in Nanda Kumar levelling charges of corruption and bribery against Hastings. However, this proved to be the death knell for Nanda Kumar. In 1774, the Supreme Court at Calcutta had been established with Sir Elijah Impey as its chief justice. Impey and Hastings went way back and enjoyed a great friendship. Working in collusion with Impey, Hastings made one of his acolytes bring about charges of forgery against Nanda Kumar, for which he was tried in the Supreme Court before a four-judge bench led by Impey in 1775. According to most accounts, the trial, which was conducted under English law, was a farce with witnesses deposing falsely and Impey acting partially. The trial merely moved towards the foregone conclusion that Nanda Kumar was to be held guilty, which he eventually was. The final act of conviction and sentencing was seen as a victory for Hastings, who was under threat of having his career ruined due to the charges levelled by Nanda Kumar.[2] One would assume that a conviction for an offence like forgery would result, at worst, in rigorous imprisonment. One would be shocked to know that the punishment for forgery under the English Common Law was a sentence of death. The dubious case of *King v. Maharaja Nanda Kumar* concluded with Nanda Kumar being sentenced to death by hanging.

After Nanda Kumar's execution, the trial against Warren Hastings and others accused of bribery and corruption ended in acquittals, as Nanda Kumar, who was the main witness, was eliminated by Warren Hastings with the help of Elijah Impey and other judges of the Supreme Court at Calcutta. Such was the effect of the conviction and execution of Nanda Kumar that many native families fled Calcutta, as inhabiting areas there would bring them under the jurisdiction of the Supreme Court and the English Common Law with regard to criminal offences prevalent in eighteenth-century England.

Under such a criminal law system, even a crime like forgery, as Nanda Kumar found out, was considered to be serious enough to merit capital punishment, which in retrospect seems exponentially disproportionate to the crime. The criminal law of England under the Common Law system in the eighteenth century prescribed capital punishment for many offences which are not considered heinous or serious under current laws. The law of crime and punishment in England at the time was labelled 'a bloody code' by Charles Smith[3] in 1857. In fact, the law against forgery, which provided for capital punishment, became the rallying point for the reform of English criminal law in the early nineteenth century, which eventually led to abolition of the death penalty for most offences in England.[4]

Common law as defined by Black's Law Dictionary means 'The body of law derived from judicial decisions, rather than from statutes or constitutions'. It was the system of law which was utilized in England for the determination of legal issues which were not covered by any statute or legislation. This meant that the judges used their own wisdom before coming to a decision without having the advantage of referring to any legislation. According to Chief Justice Hannah of the Arkansas Supreme Court, 'Common law is a judicially created law that is developed on a case by case basis.'[5] This system of law was brought to countries like the United States of America, Canada and India by the English when they colonized these countries. The opposite of a common law system would be a civil law system which means that all the laws are written by way of statutes, as opposed to common law being 'unwritten' as it is not written down by the legislature and instead relies on case laws. The legal system in India today is a balance between common law and civil law systems, as courts rely on statutes for application of law in harmony with reliance on case laws, or precedents, which leaves room for principles of equity in application of laws and protects us from rigid laws.

Being a common law country, England in the eighteenth century did not have a codification of offences and penalties but had to rely upon judicial precedents and scattered statutes for enforcement of criminal law.

Allow me to explain the difference between a code and other statutes.

A code is a bookshelf, if I may say so, containing various books on a specific subject. Only the legislature (for example, Parliament in India) has the power to add more books, remove books or edit those books on the bookshelf. The difference between a code and other statutes is the difference between a bookshelf with all the books in one place and books lying all over the place.

The term 'codification' is attributed to Jeremy Bentham,[6] the principal protagonist of this chapter. He was born on 15 February 1748 in the English countryside and went on to read law at Queen's College at Oxford University at the very young age of twelve. His age at that time probably explains why he was so afraid of ghosts, a fear which was reinforced due to the dismal surroundings of his living quarters at Oxford. He graduated with a bachelor's degree in 1763 and entered the practice of law as a barrister at Lincoln's Inn[7] in London, after which he attained his master's in 1766 from the same university. It was during his years reading law that he developed a rebellious streak. He was extremely antagonistic to the system of legislation in Common Law England and felt it to be archaic and unscientific. He was especially critical of Sir William Blackstone,[8] a legal luminary of England who was quite prominent on the lecture circuit and who went on to write famous commentaries of law. Bentham says he listened to the lectures but with rebel ears.

Bentham's career as a barrister never really took off. The main reason was that he considered the laws of England as a mountain of trash, which threw him into despair. He decided to apply himself to reform and started working on a treatise to challenge the 'lawless science of the law', the unpublished 'Critical Elements of Jurisprudence'. Bentham treated legislation both as an art and a science, as opposed to the disarray and chaos of the common law system. He worked on his writings and developed his theories at a small farm in Essex given to him by his father while living frugally on fifty pounds a year.

Bentham was of the view that the greatest possible happiness of the greatest possible numbers was the only measure of right and wrong. This was his principle of utility, or usefulness, which proposed that the good and happiness of the majority of the members of the State is the great standard by which everything related to the State must finally be determined. Thus, he was of the view that 'the greatest happiness of the greatest numbers' is the foundation of morals and legislation.[9] He believed in the principle of 'pleasure and pain', whereby the measure of good or evil was derived from the amount of pleasure or pain—physical or intellectual—brought about by an act. Bentham admittedly based his utilitarian philosophy on Joseph Priestley's 'Essay on the First Principles of Government' published in 1768, and also on the utilitarian philosophy of eighteenth-century French philosophers Claude Adrien Helvetius and Montesquieu.

Bentham believed that written law should be the only form of law, which should be clear and systematic. For this he felt that 'codification' was necessary. He wrote the 'Draught of the Code for the Organisation of Judicial Establishment in France' as a criticism of the draft on the same subject proposed by a committee of the National Assembly. In 1792, the French honoured Bentham for his writings in support of democracy and the cause of the French Revolution by bestowing him with the citizenship of France, to which Bentham responded by stating that he was a Royalist in England and a Republican in France.[10]

In 1802, the complete manuscripts of Bentham were published in French by his friend Pierre-Etienne-Louis Dumont[11] in a book called *Treatise on Legislation*[12] which was divided into 'Principles of the Civil Code' and 'Principles of the Penal Code', which had an immediate effect in England and influenced future legislation by the British Parliament. This treatise bestowed great renown upon Bentham and spread far and wide. In 1803, the Russian empress directed that the treatise be translated into Russian and wanted Bentham to codify Russian civil and penal laws. Similarly, Bentham's treatise was read avidly in Spain and formed the basis of the later amendment of Spanish laws. His work also spread to Italy, Greece and South America. If written today, his treatise would have qualified as an international bestseller. In 1810, Bentham boasted about his international celebrity in a letter to a cousin named Mulford, 'Now at length, when I am just ready to drop into the grave, my fame has spread itself all over the civilized world; and, by a selection only that was made 1802 AD, from my papers by a friend, and published in Paris, I am considered as having superseded everything that was written before me on the subject of Legislation.'

Bentham met a Scotsman by the name of James Mill[13] in or about 1808, who had been an editor of a magazine called the *Literary Journal* and a newspaper called the *St. James' Chronicle* in London. Mill was born in 1773 in Scotland in a shoemaker's family and went on to study at the University of Edinburgh. Mill is renowned for his seminal work *The History of British India,* which took ten years to write and which was published in 1817. However, Mill had never been to India and was completely ignorant about the country, its cultures and its languages. His book was later criticized to be fraught with inaccuracies due to this reason.

Bentham and Mill went on to become great friends and Mill became a disciple of Bentham and his philosophies. So much so that he named a son James Bentham, one of his nine children, after Jeremy. Bentham had also declared that he was the spiritual father of James Mill, whom he kept around as a neighbour and tenant at various points of time just to keep his company regularly. In 1819, Mill applied for a vacancy in the examiner's office at India House, the headquarters of the English East India Company. On account of his knowledge of India, and on recommendations of many of his politically influential friends, James Mill was appointed as an 'assistant to the examiner of India correspondence'. In 1821, he was appointed the second assistant, and in 1823 as the assistant examiner. Eventually, he became the 'examiner of India correspondence' in 1830, a post which he held till his death in 1836.

The influence and stature of James Mill within the East India Company and by implication to the governance of British India was underlined by Bentham when he wrote to Raja Ram Mohan Roy in 1828 informing him about Mill's desire to bring about judicial reforms in India regarding laws of evidence, criminal procedure and penal laws. He conveyed to Roy that Mill, by virtue of his closeness with the governor general, would be successful in the implementation of his plans for reform of judicial administration and procedure in India.

In the second decade of the nineteenth century, events were afoot to restrict the powers of the East India Company. The Company was stripped of its monopoly to trade with India by Parliament in 1813[14] but its political position as the government of British India had been confirmed up till 1834.

In February 1830, the British Parliament set up a committee to 'enquire into the present state of affairs of the East India Company, and into the trade between Great Britain and China'. This was in response to public demands for cessation of the powers bestowed upon the East India Company and terminating its remaining monopoly over the tea trade with China. The said committee was reconstituted twice, with James Mill being examined by the third such committee on the structure of the system which the East India Company employed for revenue collection in India, a subject which he was an expert on due to his office.

Mill was examined by the fourth committee as well, the examination being more general in nature. It was before this committee that Mill recommended the overhaul of the legislative structure for India. He suggested that a new legislative council for India should be formed comprising of four members: one expert on English law, one experienced servant of the Company, one highly qualified native and one expert on government. He also recommended the overhaul of the judicial procedure and system in India. Over and above his performance before parliamentary committees, Mill was tasked with the preparation of lengthy statements on behalf of the directors of the Company in their interactions and negotiations with the government.

The negotiations and inquiry culminated in the enactment of the Charter Act of 1833[15] which came into effect from 12 April 1834 for the period up to 12 April 1854. The Act put an end to the trading nature of the Company by winding up its commercial activities and terminating its last remaining monopoly over trade with China. The territorial possessions of the East India Company were to be held in trust for the British Crown and continued to be governed through the Board of Control. The Company, originally named the Governor and Company of Merchants of London Trading into the East Indies—which was subsequently changed to United Company of Merchants of England Trading to the East Indies in 1708 after amalgamation with a rival group of traders[16]—was officially given the name of the East India Company by way of the Charter Act of 1833.

To avoid the absolute authority of the Crown, the control of Parliament and the Board of Control through the Secret Committee was retained by the Charter. The council of the governor general was to comprise of four members, one member to solely look after legislation. It was empowered to legislate for British India, with similar powers as that of Parliament, over all persons, be they British, Indian or foreigners within the territories under the Company. However, the council could not amend or repeal the Charter Act of 1833 or encroach upon the authority of the Crown or Parliament. The British Parliament also enjoyed a concurrent power to legislate for British Indian territories.

The member nominated to look after legislation was Lord Thomas Babington Macaulay, who was a member of Parliament and the secretary of the Board of Control.[17] The creation of the position of the legislative member was done in line with the recommendations made by James Mill, who wanted a person well versed in the ways of men and philosophy to be a part of the council. Though Macaulay was nominated by the government, the power to appoint him rested with the directors of the East India Company. The chairman and deputy chairman of the Company were very unhappy with the nomination as Macaulay had been one of the foremost critics of the Company and had delivered a monumental speech when the Charter Act was being discussed in the Parliament.[18] However, they based their opposition on the fact that Macaulay was just thirty-three at the time and therefore too young for the job.[19]

Macaulay was an advocate for termination of the trading activities of the East India Company and was of the view that, 'The existence of such a body as this gigantic corporation, this political monster of two natures, subject in one hemisphere, sovereign in another, had never been contemplated by the legislators or judges of former ages.' Even though he advocated the termination of the Company's trading activities, he still felt it would be desirable to retain the Company as an organ of the British government over India. While lamenting on the lack of democratic form of government in India:

Macaulay was scathing in his criticism of James Mill. He said:

> One gentleman, extremely well acquainted with the affairs of our Eastern Empire, a most valuable servant of the Company, and the author of a History of India, which, though not certainly free from faults, is, I think, on the whole, the greatest historical work which has appeared in our language since that of Gibson—I mean Mr Mill—was examined on this point. That gentleman is well known to be very bold and uncompromising politician. He has written strongly, far too strongly, I think, in favour of pure democracy. He has gone so far as to maintain that no nation which has not a representative legislature, chosen by universal suffrage, enjoys security against oppression. But when he was asked before the Committee of last year whether he thought representative government practicable in India, his answer was, 'Utterly out of the Question.' This then is the state in which we are. We have to frame a good government for a country into which, by universal acknowledgment, we cannot introduce those institutions which all our habits, which all the reasonings of European philosophers, which all the history of our own part

of the world would lead us to consider as the one
great security for good government.

It is quite clear that Macaulay and Mill weren't really
the best of friends; in fact Macaulay referred to Mill as
an old enemy. It was to James Mill that the directors of
the Company deferred to on the question of Macaulay's
appointment, imagining he would support them in their
opposition. However, to the directors' and Macaulay's
surprise, Mill recommended that Macaulay would be
an excellent choice for the position, and if they rejected
him they would hardly be able to find a better person for
the role. This magnanimity resulted in the repairing of
their relationship, and Macaulay in fact consulted Mill
on occasion before starting with his role in India.[20] The
directors of the East India Company eventually appointed
Macaulay to the position with nineteen directors voting in
his favour and three against.[21]

Having bestowed the council with legislative power, the
Charter Act of 1833 provided the council with the assistance
of a commission for legal reform in India so that the laws of
India may be formed into a code. Macaulay, in his speech,
said:

I believe no country has ever stood so much need
of a code of laws as India; and I believe, also that
there never was a country in which the want might
so easily be supplied. I said that there were many
points of analogy between the state of that country,
after the fall of the Mogul power, and the state of
Europe after the fall of the Roman empire. . . . As
there were in Europe then, so there are in India
now, several systems of law, widely differing
from each other, but coexisting and coequal. The

indigenous population has its own law. Each of the successive races of conquerors has brought with it its own peculiar jurisprudence . . . so we have now in our Eastern empire Hindoo law, Mahometan law, Parsee law, English law, perpetually mingling with each other and disturbing each other, varying with person, varying with the place. . . . The only Mahometan book in the nature of a code is the Koran; the only Hindoo book the Institutes.[22] Everybody who knows those books knows that they provide for a very small part of the cases which must arise in every community.

He echoed Bentham, Mill and other advocates of codification when he said, 'Our principle is simply this: uniformity where you can have it; diversity where you must have it; but in all cases certainty.' This was a break from the common law system and judge-made laws. This principle is the driving force behind modern Indian legislation till date.[23]

3

The Indian Penal Code and Sedition

The first Indian Law Commission was formed under the chairpersonship of Thomas Macaulay in accordance with the Charter Act of 1833. The other members of the commission were John M. Macleod, G.W. Anderson, F. Millett and Charles H. Cameron. As a measure of reform of Indian criminal law, Macaulay wrote a proposal to the governor general recommending the preparation of a penal code which would not merely be a digest of existing customs and regulations but would also be reformatory in nature and framed on the basis of two principles. One, the principle of suppressing crime with the smallest account of suffering, and two, the principle of ascertaining truth at the smallest possible cost of time and money.[1]

The government accepted the proposal and ordered the commencement of drafting the penal code on 15 June 1835. However, the commission's work was hindered by the protracted ill health of Charles H. Cameron and the absence of G.W. Anderson from Calcutta for long stretches of time. Only Millett somewhat assisted Macaulay, and that too only when he was available, which by Macaulay's account was not enough. Such unfortunate circumstances led to the responsibility of drafting the penal code lying largely with Macaulay, and therefore, he should be considered the true author of the same. The draft penal code was completed after two years in 1837, making Macaulay defensive of the delay.

In a letter dated 2 January 1837, Macaulay pointed out that the drafting of the French Criminal Code began in 1801 but the Code of Criminal Procedure and Penal Code was only completed in 1808 and 1810, respectively. This delay occurred even though Napoleon had many jurists at his disposal, as compared to Macaulay single-handedly drafting the Indian code. He also compared the time taken to draft the code with the four-and-a-half years taken to draft the Criminal Code of Louisiana[2] which had commenced in 1821.

The draft penal code was finally presented to Lord George Auckland, the governor general, on 14 October 1837 with an introductory report and detailed notes on the various chapters of the draft code containing illustrations and examples.

In drafting the penal code, the commission did not follow any existing system of law in India even though it conducted an inquiry into the existing system of indigenous penal laws.[3] The report noted that the Hindu penal laws had long been discarded by Indian rulers in favour of Muslim penal laws, which had in turn been largely modified by British Regulations. The Bombay Presidency had in fact completely discarded indigenous laws and relied on English law. The Bengal, Madras and Bombay Presidencies at that time had a different set of regulations altogether, which provided different punishments for similar offences.

The Bombay Presidency had Regulation XIV of 1827 as a compendium of offences and punishments, as opposed to various regulations in the Madras and Bengal Presidencies. However, the commission was especially critical of the

Bombay Regulations and did not consider it fit enough to be relied upon to draft the penal code. Its main criticism arose from the fact that the penal laws of the Bombay Presidency prescribed disproportionate punishments even for varying degrees of the same offence. As an example, punishment for destruction of property worth just one rupee also attracted a punishment of five years' imprisonment, the same as punishment for much greater destruction. Another criticism was that unequal offences were often punished equally. For example, the punishment for concealment of a murder was the same as that for committing murder. The commission found the mechanism of categorization of offences and penalties to be completely unscientific and arbitrary.

However, the commission did rely upon the French Penal Code and decisions of French Courts as well as the Penal Code of Louisiana which was also based on the French Code.

The draft penal code did not specify the territorial application of the code as it felt that it would be a political question and would depend on treaty relations between native rulers and the British. However, the commission was of the opinion that the code should apply to everyone within the British Indian territory as well as to the princely states. It recommended that the penal code should immediately be made applicable to the mofussil[4] and translated versions of the code be provided to the natives to enable them to understand the penal law in the vernacular.

The draft penal code contained twenty-six chapters[5] concerning, among others, punishments; general exceptions; offences relating to the State, armed forces, public justice, revenue, coin, religion or caste, illicit immigration and residence, press, body, property, marriage, and defamation; abuse of powers by public servants; contempt of lawful authority of public servants; illegal pursuit of legal rights;

and criminal breach of contracts of service.[6] The provisions were divided into 488 clauses.

Chapter V of the draft penal code enumerated the act which could amount to offences against the State. The State here referred to the government of the territories of the East India Company and not the British Crown. This was clarified by the Law Commission in its notes on the said chapter.

Clause 113 of the draft code stated what would constitute the offence of sedition:

> Whoever, by words, either spoken or intended to be read, or by signs, or by visible representation, attempts to excite feelings of disaffection to the Government established by law in the territories of the East India Company, among any class of people who live under that Government, shall be punished with banishment for life or for any other term from the territories of the East India Company, to which fine may be added, or with simple imprisonment for a term which may extend to three years, to which fine may be added, or with fine.
>
> Explanation—Such a disapprobation of the measures of the Government as is compatible with a disposition to render obedience to the lawful authority of the Government, and to support the lawful authority of the Government against unlawful attempts to subvert or resist that authority, is not disaffection. Therefore the making of comments on the measures of the Government, with the intention of exciting only this species of disapprobation, is not an offence within this Clause.

Though the Law Commission did not mention the word 'sedition' in Clause 113, it did clarify in its notes on the chapter titled 'Defamation' that imputations intended to inflame the people against the government would be punishable as sedition under Clause 113. It also clarified that an attack made on the public administration of the governor of a presidency would not be seditious if it is made in good faith.

The provision on sedition was based on the Libel Act of 1792 enacted in England, and the law settled after that.[7] The term 'sedition' is derived from the Latin word *seditio* which translates into 'riot'. However, sedition in its usage under English law[8] did not actually mean an act, unlike rioting. Sedition was categorized as a class of offences against internal public peace not accompanied by or leading to open violence. In fact, there was no such offence of 'sedition' known to English law. Rather than have a single offence called sedition, seditious offences were categorized as seditious words, seditious libels and seditious conspiracies.

To understand the background of the law, it is necessary to understand the term 'libel'. Words when published in print with the intention to wrongfully raise imputations against the character of a person to defame them amounts to 'libel'. In the context of sedition, such wrongful imputations of defamatory character when made against the government or monarch could amount to seditious libel.

The first definitive statement of law on any offence of the likes of sedition was mentioned in the First Statute of Westminster of 1275 which was enacted by an assembly called by King Edward I of England, who had just returned from the last great crusade and ascended to the throne of England in 1272. At the beginning of the half-century reign of King Edwards's father, King Henry III, there was complete disorder and lawlessness in England. The biggest reason for such disorder was the non-compatibility of the races inhabiting England, which included the Normans,[9] Saxons[10] and Celts,[11] etc. The Saxons and Celts had inhabited England long before the Norman conquest of 1066 but were thereafter ruled by the Normans, who were considered foreigners, and the English Crown was seen as being occupied by aliens. The assimilation of the Normans and Saxons began in the twelfth and thirteenth centuries and the desire for a common English tongue and laws arose during the reign of King Henry. However, Henry was a weak leader and could not impose his will upon his people. In fact, in 1263, common Londoners had thrown stones at Queen Eleanor when she was commuting between palaces—such was the lack of respect for the Crown in England at that time. When Edward was officially crowned in 1274, it was down to him to bring about a semblance of organization and law and order in his kingdom. King Edward I was credited with a 'legislative mind' and was later responsible for the first statute for the formation of the first modern Parliament in England in 1295 which comprised of all the lords of the land. However, the first Assembly, similar to the modern Parliament, was convened by King Edward in 1275 at Westminster in the above-mentioned background of Norman–Saxon assimilation and the need for regulation by law of the state of affairs in his kingdom. This Assembly enacted the Statute of Westminster which sought to correct abuses, cure defects and remodel the administration of justice. The statute was later described to be more in the nature of a code than a simple Act of Parliament.[12] Clause 34 of the Statute provided:[13]

> For as much as there have been often times found in the country [devisers] of tales whereby discord or occasion of discord has many time arisen between the King and his people or great men of this realm for the damage that hath and may therefore ensue, it is commanded that from henceforth none be so

hardy to cite or publish any false news or tales whereby discord or slander may grow between the King and his people or the great men of the realm; and he that doth so shall be taken and kept in prison until he hath brought him into the court which was the first author of the tale.

In simple words, people were prohibited from speaking or publishing false news or stories which could bring about discord between the king and his subjects, and such false news and stories which were slanderous of the king and the 'great men' of the kingdom. Anyone who did so was to be imprisoned, and a burden was placed on such people to bring forward the original author of the false story to face the court. It was noteworthy that the provision sought to only punish false news and stories and not everything critical published or spoken against the king. Clause 34 lived on for more than 600 years till it was repealed in 1887 by the Statute Law Revision Act! However, prior to the Libel Act of 1792, there was no specific statute governing seditious libel. Before that, trials of a political nature were held before the Star Chambers, which was established in the mid-fifteenth century and comprised of privy councillors, who were the king's advisers, and judges who used Common Law to punish critical discussions on political affairs as seditious libel. The Star Chambers' proceedings were arbitrary, secretive and oppressive. At the turn of the eighteenth century, there was a shift in public sentiment against political libel, and the powers of English judges were restricted by the Libel Act of 1792, which restricted the prosecution of seditious libel to cases where there was a direct incitement to crimes against the government.[14]

Similarity to this law could be found in the Book Licencing Act of 1662 in England, which remained in force up till 1694. This was when printing and publishing of books was just taking off. The Act mandated that books could only be published under a licence, and heretical, seditious or offensive content against the Christian faith, the Church of England, the State or the Commonwealth could not be published. However, the offence was classified as a misdemeanour and not a grave crime.[15]

Even the French Penal Code contained provisions concerning seditious acts which made actions critical of the government, president or any public authority of the French Republic punishable under the code. Articles published in the press containing criticism of public authorities for their public conduct also attracted penalties.[16]

The term of the first Indian Law Commission ended in 1838 with the draft code staying in draft form. It was circulated to the Supreme Courts of the presidencies for their views, and thereafter the comments were taken up for consideration by the Law Commission led by Charles H. Cameron, who was also a member of the first Law Commission but unable to contribute much due to ill health. The revised draft penal code was submitted to the government in 1847. One of the criticisms that the draft code received was that it was not codification in the technical sense as it attempted to change the entire criminal jurisprudence of India which was otherwise based on indigenous laws. Sir H. Compton, the chief justice of the Bombay Supreme Court at that time, therefore felt that the Law Commission had exceeded its brief. The further revised draft code was submitted to the British Indian government in 1851.[17]

At this stage, the draft code met opposition from John Elliot Drinkwater Bethune,[18] who was appointed as the legislative member of the Governor General's Council in 1849. He prepared another draft penal code of his own which completely differed from Macaulay's draft and was contrary to the Benthamite principles employed by Macaulay. Bethune's draft code was based on the orthodox criminal laws of England in language as well as substance. Lord Dalhousie, the governor general, rather than decide the difference of opinion between the Law Commission and J.E.D. Bethune, himself referred the issue to the government in England. The British government reiterated its position in 1854, based on the recommendation of the Law Commission, that the draft penal code prepared by the first Law Commission under Macaulay should be revised and enacted at the earliest without much alteration in phraseology and framework.[19] However, the enactment of the penal code was left pending as the legislative process moved at a glacial pace.

The events of a few years later spurred the British back into action. These events are collectively known as the Sepoy Mutiny or the Revolt of 1857. By that time there was major public discontent against the rule of the East India Company because of the economic exploitation of the natives. British land and revenue policies resulted in the impoverishment of both peasants and landlords (zamindars) alike. In addition to that, the police and petty officials were extremely corrupt which furthered the discontent against the establishment. The British in 1856 declared that Bahadur Shah would be the last Mughal emperor of India, and his successors would only be recognized as princes. He was also asked to vacate the Red Fort in Delhi, which was the seat of power of the Mughal Empire. Another major reason for discontent among the masses, and especially the sepoys, was the propagation of Christianity by missionaries and British officers. Add to that the taxation of land on which Hindu temples and Muslim mosques stood, and the natives were convinced that the British were out to destroy their religion.[20]

In the lead-up to the revolt, the British annexed Oudh (Awadh)[21] in 1856, which did not go down well with the

Company's sepoys, the majority of whom came from Oudh. Apart from Oudh, the British were on a campaign to annex other princely states, including Jhansi, Nagpur, Satara and Sambalpur. This caused concern among the native rulers who feared losing their realms. Indians were also kept out of administrative and legislative positions in the East India Company which resulted in a lack of understanding of local customs, usages and aspirations of the people. However, the most proximate cause of the revolt was the introduction of the Enfield rifle which replaced the old muskets the sepoys were using.[22]

The new rifles required a special kind of cartridge which had to be bitten off at its ends before being used. These cartridges were greased by lard made from the fat of pigs and cows. Eating the meat of pigs was prohibited for Muslims, and eating beef was prohibited for Hindus. The sepoys raised their concerns with the government, which failed to allay their suspicion that it continued using pig and cow fat for the grease. Though sepoys conducted acts of defiance in February, the real spark for the mutiny occurred on 29 March 1857 when Mangal Pandey, a sepoy of the 34th Bengal Native Infantry, openly mutinied in Barrackpur.[23] Thereafter, the infantry was disbanded, and the sepoys returned to their native Oudh and spread the word about the mutiny. This resulted in multiple mutinies in places like Delhi, Ambala and Lucknow. The mutiny was followed by a civilian uprising which spread across north India. Bahadur Shah was declared the emperor of India by the rebels who took control of the Red Fort and Delhi. However, by September of 1857, British troops took back control of Delhi and recaptured the Red Fort on 20 September 1857 with Bahadur Shah surrendering the next day.[24] The revolt lasted till July 1859 with multiple battles between the British and various native forces.

The British Parliament and the Crown laid the blame for the revolt on the East India Company and enacted the Government of India Act of 1858 by which the government of India was transferred to the British Crown, and the properties of the Company vested in the Crown. The Board of Control and the Court of Directors of the Company were replaced by a secretary of state with a council of fifteen members to assist him. The governor general became a direct representative of the Crown and governed with the help of his council.[25]

The transfer of power to the Crown hastened the legislative process and made the enactment of the penal code imperative considering the revolt, as the British had consolidated their position in India by then and controlled almost all of the Indian subcontinent either as sovereign or in alliance with native rulers. The legislative member of the governor general's council at that time was Barnes Peacock, an English barrister who went on to become the chief justice of the Supreme Court of Calcutta.[26] He was tasked with the revision and enactment of the dormant draft penal code. The draft code underwent revision at the hands of the Legislative Council[27] and received the assent of the governor general on 6 October 1860 and was supposed to come into effect from 1 May 1861.[28] However, the effective date of the penal code was deferred to 1 January 1862, to allow the judges and administrators in India more time to study the code.[29]

Thomas Macaulay, the rightful author of the draft Indian penal code, could not witness its enactment as he passed away on 28 December 1859, just under a year before the IPC was enacted.[30]

James F. Stephen (more on him later in this chapter) described the IPC as the criminal law of England freed from all technicalities and superfluities, systematically arranged and modified to suit British India.[31] He blamed the delay on the reluctance of the British Indian government to interfere with native institutions, and attributed the credit for the passage of the IPC to Barnes Peacock, who improved the draft code with practical skill and technical knowledge through a period described as the most anxious that the British Empire in India had witnessed. He commended Macaulay for the gift of going to the root of the matter in preparing such a detailed code despite being a barrister who barely practiced criminal law, or any law for that matter.[32]

Oddly, the IPC did not have a provision for the offence of sedition, which was present in the draft code as Clause 113. However, it retained provisions under the chapter on offences against the State.

This situation attracted the attention of James Fitzjames Stephen, an English Cambridge-educated barrister, who was appointed as the legislative member of the Governor General's Council in 1869. He went on to become a judge of the Calcutta High Court in 1879. In fact, Stephen had also been offered the chief justice's position at the Calcutta High Court in 1869 upon the same being vacated by Barnes Peacock. However, Stephen chose to accept the position in the Council instead. Stephen was responsible for, among others, the drafting and enactment of the Indian Evidence Act of 1872, the Indian Contract Act of 1872, and the revision of the Criminal Procedure Code in 1872, which had originally been enacted in 1862 to supplement the IPC.[33] He noted the absence of the provision against sedition and thought it fit to be brought back into the fold of the IPC.[34]

The lack of provisions criminalizing offences against the State had earlier forced the British Indian government to enact the State Offences Act in May 1857 after the outbreak of the revolt. The Act provided for the prevention, trial and punishment of offences against the State, without defining what such offences entailed. The governments of the presidencies were empowered to try the commission of offences against the State, as well as the offences of murder, arson, robbery or other heinous crime against person or property.[35] Judgments of the special courts which tried such offences were final and non-appealable.[36] Only natives could be tried under the Act as natural-born subjects of the British Crown were explicitly exempted from the provisions of the Act.[37]

The more immediate need for enactment of the provision against sedition may have arisen because of the Wahhabi Movement. Wahhabis are Muslims who believe in monotheism (one God) and jihad (waging of war when no other means remain) for protection of Islam. They oppose the belief that saints and seers are nearer to God than ordinary Muslims, and are against practices like the worship of saints and tombs. They are followers of Muhammad bin Abdul Wahab, who along with Amir Mohammed Bin Saud, the founder of the House of Saud, gave birth to Wahhabism in Saudi Arabia. The Indian Wahhabi Movement was started by one Syed Ahmed of Bareilly[38] in the third decade of the nineteenth century. Originally, the movement was against the Sikh empire in northwest India, but after the British defeated the Sikhs in 1849 the movement turned into the most anti-British movement in India. Wahhabis infiltrated the British army in many parts of India and attempted to indoctrinate others through letters and personal contact. Though the Wahhabis campaigned against the British throughout the revolt of 1857, they did not join the general movement but continued their separate campaign. The British discovered a conspiracy in 1863, which spread from Patna[39] to the North West Frontier[40] via Ambala,[41] to supply manpower and money to the Wahhabis to fight the British in the North-West Frontier Province. This led to the trial and transportation for life of notable Wahhabi figures in Ambala (1864) and Patna (1865). Though the trials significantly weakened the Wahhabi Movement, it still did not die but continued in the provinces of Bengal and Bihar and parts of the Madras and Bombay Presidencies till 1882.[42]

After the Ambala and Patna trials, a need was felt by the British Indian government to amend the IPC to provide for seditious offences not amounting to waging war, or attempt or abetment to wage war, against the British Crown. Inquiries were held into the activities of the Wahhabis in Bombay and Bengal. Aravind Ganachari quotes Ashley Eden, secretary to the Judicial Department of the British Indian government, 'There can be no doubt that where a population is at once ignorant and fanatical, as are the Mohammedans of India, seditious teachings are to be made a substantive offence.'[43]

One of the most complete descriptions of the sedition law at the time was laid down by Justice Fitzgerald in 1868[44] while trying a case against two journalists for publishing seditious writings. These writings were published at the time of the Fenian Rising of 1867 when the Irish led by the Irish Republican Brotherhood rebelled violently against British Rule in Ireland. Justice Fitzgerald, in laying the charge before the jury, said, 'Sedition in itself is a comprehensive term and it embraces all those practices, whether by word, deed or writing, which are calculated to disturb the tranquillity of the State, and lead ignorant persons to endeavour to subvert the Government and the laws of the Empire. The objects of sedition generally are to induce discontent and insurrection and to stir up opposition to the Government, and bring the administration of justice into contempt; and the very tendency of sedition is to incite the people to insurrection and rebellion.' He went on to say, 'Sedition has been described as disloyalty in action, and the law considers as sedition all those practices which have for their object to excite discontent or dissatisfaction; to create public disturbance, or to lead to civil war; to bring into hatred or contempt the Sovereign or the Government, the laws or constitution of the realm and, generally all endeavours to promote public disorder.'

Justice Fitzgerald, however, qualified the charge by saying, 'Journalists are entitled to criticize the conduct and intentions of those entrusted with the administration of the Government. They are entitled to canvass and, if necessary, censure either the acts or proceedings of Parliament, and are entitled to point out any grievances under which the people labour.' He concluded that, 'When a public writer exceeds his limit, and uses his privilege to create discontent and dissatisfaction, he becomes guilty of what the law calls sedition.' Therefore, he created an exception for cases where criticism and disapproval of the government, however severe, does not amount to sedition if it's a part of free and fair discussion which does not excite disaffection against the government.

On 25 November 1870, the Legislative Council of the governor general led by Stephen amended the IPC by Act XXVII of 1870 and introduced section 124A, which was a revised version of Clause 113 of the draft penal code.

Section 124A was inserted between Section 124 (assaulting President, Governor, etc. with intent to compel or restrain the exercise of any lawful power) and Section 125 (waging war against any Asiatic power in alliance with the Government of India) of the Indian Penal Code. The original Section 124A read as:

Whoever by words either spoken or intended to be read or by signs or by visible representation or otherwise excites or attempts to excite feelings of disaffection to the Government established by law in British India shall be punished with transportation for life or for any term to which fine may be added or with imprisonment for a term which may extend to three years to which fine may be added or with fine.

Explanation—Such a disapprobation of the measures of the Government as is compatible with a disposition to render obedience to the lawful authority of the Government, and to support the lawful authority against unlawful attempts to subvert or resist that authority is not disaffection. Therefore, the making of comments on the measures of the Government with the intention of exciting only this species of disapprobation is not an offence within this clause.

Within the complicated language of the explanation, the section created a category of actions which would not amount to sedition. The explanation left a lot to be desired and did not help in curing the vagueness and breadth of the original provision. The courts were left to determine the applicability of the provision with guidance from decisions of British courts on each aspect of the provision.

After the enactment, Stephen asserted that the law on sedition was substantially the same as the law of England at that time, though it was more concise and explicit and thus free from the obscurity and vagueness with which the English law on sedition suffered. In explaining the omission of Clause 113 of the draft code from the IPC, Stephen referred to a letter he had received from Barnes Peacock wherein he stated that the exclusion had been a mistake even though he had drawn up a revised Clause 113. He could not recollect why the clause was omitted but attributed the·

omission to oversight. He further emphasized the need for the enactment of Section 124A as he felt that in the absence of a specific provision in the IPC for sedition, the provisions of the Treason Felony Act of 1848 would be attracted. By virtue of Section 3 of the Treason Felony Act, even the mere thought or conception of committing a seditious act against the British Crown was punishable by transportation for life. This was the more severe of the two provisions as Section 124A only published seditious words or writings and not just mere thought.[45]

After the coming into force of Section 124A of the IPC, the British Indian government enacted two preventive laws to supplement Section 124A. The first was the Dramatic Performances Act of 1876 intended to prevent performances of a seditious, defamatory or scandalous nature. Though offences such as sedition, defamation, etc., were punishable after their occurrence, the government wanted to even prevent the staging of plays which would give rise to commission of such offences and would be likely to lead to breach of peace. According to Donogh, a play by the name of *Chai Ka Darpan* was the most proximate cause for enactment of this law. The play portrayed owners of tea plantations and promoters of migration to tea-growing districts as evil persons who exploited migrants, both physically and sexually.

Now, if there is one rule that you don't break, it's that you do not mess with the Englishman's tea.

Angered by the attack on the honour of tea planters, the British thought it necessary to prevent such plays in future and issued an ordinance enabling the Bengal government to prohibit and prevent such plays in future. The Dramatic Performances Act was based on this ordinance. Prosecution under the Dramatic Performances Act did not bar separate prosecution under section 124A of the IPC.[46]

Interestingly, the Dramatic Performances Act was not repealed by the Indian Parliament after Independence and various states continued to employ the Act to censor plays. The Government of India finally repealed the Dramatic Performances Act of 1876 by way of the Repeal and Amending (Second) Act, 2017.

Another preventive measure by the British Indian government was the Vernacular Press Act of 1878. It was enacted to place newspapers published in local languages under the control of the government for repressing seditious writings which are intended to produce disaffection towards the government in the minds of natives. Newspapers printed in vernacular languages were published in most of the large towns in Bengal, Bombay, North-West Frontier Province and Punjab and enjoyed a wide circulation. The government felt that Section 124A was not sufficient to punish writings in the nature of seditious libel in the vernacular press which incited people to upset the British Raj and cast aspersions on the government by alleging tyranny and injustice. The British Indian government sought to curb such activities by introducing censorship and thus prevention of probable seditious libel from appearing in the vernacular press.

One of the advocates for the introduction of the Act was the aforementioned Ashley Eden, who had by then risen to the position of lieutenant governor of Bengal. The Act provided for publishers of the vernacular newspapers and periodicals to deposit monetary security as an undertaking not to publish seditious writings, and the security stood forfeited as penalty if there was a breach of the undertaking. Further, it provided for temporary supervision of the publication by the government in case the publisher did not want to furnish any security. The Vernacular Press Act was a short-lived statute which was repealed in 1881.[47]

James F. Stephen published a digest of criminal laws for England in 1877 which was intended to be the draft criminal code of England. This digest also provided for the offence of sedition but divided the offence into two parts as opposed to the singular provision in the IPC. The first part as stated in Article 96 of the digest provided for the offence of 'seditious words and libels'. The second part created an offence of 'seditious conspiracy' under Article 97 of the digest. Both the provisions mandated the presence of 'seditious intention' for either of the acts to be an offence. Stephen defined 'seditious intention' under Article 98, which was more or less similar to Section 124A of the IPC. Article 99 of the digest provided for 'presumption as to intention' for determining seditious intention. It stated that the intention of seditious libel or conspiracy would be presumed to be the bringing about of consequences which would naturally flow from such actions.

The creation of distinction between types of seditious offences and the definition of intention as provided by Stephen could have easily been brought into the IPC by the British Indian government, but they did not do so. Such an amendment would have clarified the law on the subject which otherwise suffered from ambiguities. James F. Stephen's digest of criminal laws was turned into a draft Criminal Code for England, but the British Parliament failed to enact it into law. Attempts have been made by the British Parliament till recently to codify their criminal law, but they have only met with failure.

PART II

EARLY LIFE

4

Four Trials and an Amendment

From the time Section 124A was inserted into the IPC there was no prosecution or trial under the section for twenty-one years until 1891.

In the meantime, nationalist movements were gaining ground in the Bengal and Bombay Presidencies. Organizations like the Arya Samaj[1] and Brahmo Samaj[2] were championing the cause of Hindu nationalism which, as opposed to the Wahhabi Movement, wanted a Hindu nation with place for all religions. In 1867, an annual gathering called the Hindu Mela[3] was started in Calcutta to promote national feeling, a sense of patriotism and spirit of self-help among Hindus. The event was used to assert Hindu nationalism and exhibit pan-Indian indigenous arts and crafts, and was organized for thirteen years till 1880. It saw the emergence of Rabindranath Tagore, who as a boy of eighteen recited patriotic songs and poems at the event in 1879. The Arya Samaj was promoting political independence through the ideas of swaraj[4] and swadeshi[5] before the terms became fashionable.[6]

On the other hand, Surendra Nath Banerji, a former Indian Civil Service officer who was dismissed by the

British in 1874, was mobilizing the students and youth of Bengal with his lectures on nationalism. He had started fomenting anti-British feelings. He moved the discourse of the nationalist movement in Bengal towards political nationalism and away from religious nationalism. He also introduced the message of Giuseppe Mazzini to Bengal. Mazzini had spearheaded a movement for a republican-unified Italy in the mid-nineteenth century through a secret organization called the Young Italy Movement and was opposed to the Austrian occupation of Italy. On the west coast, Mahadev Govind Ranade, who was a sub-judge in the service of the British, made a deep study of the economic problems which India was facing at the time. He was an advocate for the industrial and commercial development of India, towards which he set up the Industrial Association of Western India in 1890.[7]

By 1875, there were about 475 newspapers in circulation in Bengal, mostly in vernacular languages. Organized political movements started in Bengal with the establishment of the Indian Association by Surendra Nath Banerji in 1876. In 1878, Banerji toured the Bombay and the Madras Presidencies to influence public opinion against British policies in India. The Vernacular Press Act of 1878, which was discussed in the previous chapter, was enacted by the British government as a reaction to the shift in public opinion against British rule in India. However, the incoming governor general, Lord Ripon, repealed the Vernacular Press Act in 1882 and brought about a bill for the improvement of local self-government in 1883 which attempted to remove the bar on Indian magistrates trying cases involving English and European defendants. However, the Anglo-Indians (the English and Europeans who lived in India then) succeeded in thwarting the Bill. This made the Indians realize that the opposition to the bill was based on the concept of racial superiority. Banerji was even imprisoned for two months for criticizing the Calcutta High Court, which caused public unrest and rioting. His absence weakened the Indian agitation for passage of the bill. His imprisonment attracted sympathy from all quarters and even from far-off provinces in the Madras and Bombay Presidencies.[8]

After his release, a national political conference was organized in 1883 in Calcutta led by Surendra Nath Banerji which was attended by both Hindu and Muslim delegates from across India. This was followed by the establishment of the Bombay Presidency Association in 1885. Prior to this, the Madras Mahajana Sabha, which held a provincial conference in 1881, had been established. Indians realized the need for a pan-Indian organization to further their political goals which in turn led to the convening of the first Indian National Congress in Pune by Allan Octavian Hume in December 1885. The meeting was attended by delegates who were politicians from all parts of the Bengal, Bombay and Madras Presidencies. However, the first meeting could not be held in Pune because of an outbreak of cholera and it was shifted to Bombay. This was a watershed moment in Indian history: the birth of the organized freedom movement in India.[9]

The first trial under Section 124A took place in this backdrop in 1891 when the vernacular press had grown assertive and Indian nationalism was on the rise.

Age-old misogynistic systems against women were going through a change in the nineteenth century in India. The abolition of sati[10] in 1829, the legalization of widow remarriage in 1856, and the prohibition of female infanticide in 1870 were some of the steps taken by the British government in India towards social reform aimed at ancient practices which victimized women. At that time, the socio-religious Hindu practice was to have girl children married to older men by the tender age of ten, and they were obligated to be impregnated within sixteen days of the wedding under a custom called *garbhadaan*, which literally means donating the womb. However, instead of challenging such a patriarchal system, activists of the day looked towards reformation of the system to enable a girl to reach physical maturity which would be just enough for garbhadaan while not harming her health. The IPC as enacted in 1860 had provided various ages for 'intelligent consent' for offences committed upon a person, ranging from ten to twelve to sixteen years. For statutory rape under Section 375[11] of the IPC the age of consent was fixed at ten years, but this was not extended to marital rape in compliance with socio-religious realities of the day.[12]

The otherwise reluctant British government, which did not want to offend its Hindu subjects, was forced into action by the death of a child bride, Phoolmani, who was all of ten years old in 1889. She was married to a man named Hari Mohan Maiti who was over thirty years of age. Hari Mohan had sexual intercourse with her on their wedding night which allegedly led to her death that night itself. Hari Mohan was consequently charged for her rape and murder, and the case led to the coinage of the term 'Harimaitism' for the practice of consummation of marriage with child brides. Unfortunately, Hari Mohan was acquitted of the charge of rape by the court because the law against rape did not apply to the marital rape of a girl ten years of age.[13]

The British government enacted the Age of Consent Act on 19 March 1891, which amended Section 375 and raised the age of consent from ten to twelve years, thus making sexual intercourse with any girl below the age of twelve, whether with or without her consent, an offence amounting to rape. This law was religion-neutral and applied to all native communities in British India.[14]

A vernacular by the name of *Bangobasi* was a weekly newspaper which had a large circulation in Bengal; its name meant 'Citizen of Bengal'. On 26 March 1891, the newspaper published the first of five articles attacking the Age of Consent Act as being opposed to Hindu traditions and morality. A translated extract of the first offending article goes:[15]

> The English ruler is our lord and master, and can interfere with our religion and usages by brute force and European civilization. The Hindu is powerless to resist; but he is superior to your nation in good morals, in gentle conduct and in good education. Hindu civilization and the Hindu religion are in danger of being destroyed. The Englishman stands revealed in his true colours. He has a rifle and bayonet and slanders the Hindu from the might of the gun. How are we to conciliate him? We cannot expect mercy or justice from him. Our chief fear is that religion will be destroyed, but the Hindu religion nevertheless remains unshaken. We suffer from the ravages of famine, from inundations, from the oppressive delays of the law courts, from accidents on steamers and railways. All these misfortunes have become more prevalent with the extension of English rule in India; but our rulers do not attempt to remove these troubles or to ameliorate our condition. All their compassion is expended in removing the imaginary grievances of girl-wives and interfering with our customs. We should freely vent our real grievances. We are unable to rebel, but we are not of those who say it would be improper to do so if we could. We have been conquered by brute force, but we are superior to the English in ethics

and morality, in which we have nothing to learn from them. You may crush the body but you cannot affect the mind. Others like Aurungzebe and Kalapahar have tried before you and failed. You should not try and suppress girl-marriage because you won at Plassey and Assaye. It is error and presumption on your part to attempt to reform our morals.

As a consequence of publication of the offending articles, the proprietor, editor, manager and printer of *Bangobasi* were all charged by the government for sedition under Section 124A before the Calcutta High Court in the famous case known as *Queen Empress v. Jogendra Chunder Bose & Ors.*[16]

The defence argued that only the actual writer of seditious libel could be prosecuted under Section 124A, and not the publisher and others who helped in publication of the writing in question. This was based on the fact that Section 124A as originally enacted did not mention that even the publication of seditious writing by anyone other than the original author would amount to an offence. In the present case, the identity of the author of the article in question was unknown. The defence further argued that the defendants could not be made criminally liable for the acts of the author, who was merely their agent. The defence relied on an English judgment[17] to substantiate its arguments. Justice C. Petheram, the chief justice of the Calcutta High Court, negated this submission and stated that the essence of Section 124A was the attempt to excite disaffection by words intended to be read, and did not restrict the scope of the offence to the writer alone. Therefore, anyone, including the publisher, who uses such seditious writing to excite disaffection as provided under Section 124A was liable for punishment for sedition.

The defence then argued that the articles published in *Bangobasi* did not contain any direct incitement to rebellion or use of force against the British government and therefore did not exceed the bounds of legitimate criticism. However, Justice Petheram felt that comparisons with 'tyrants' like Aurangzeb[18] and Kalapahad[19] was bound to cause feelings of hatred and enmity against the British government which could have resulted in violence.

Justice Petheram summarized the charge to the jury and placed two issues before them. Firstly, they had to understand what an offence under Section 124A would be, and secondly, based on that understanding and the evidence produced before them, they had to determine if the accused were guilty of sedition. He further explained that the words 'disaffection' and 'disapprobation' in Section 124A were not synonymous as contended by the defence. He was of the opinion that whenever the prefix 'dis' is added to a word, the word formed conveys an idea which would be the opposite of whatever would be conveyed by the word without the prefix. Therefore, he believed that disaffection meant a feeling contrary to affection which would amount to dislike or hatred. On the other hand, he believed that disapprobation meant mere disapproval. He summarized:

> If a person uses either spoken or written words calculated to create in the minds of the persons to whom they are addressed a disposition not to obey the lawful authority of the Government, or to subvert or resist that authority, if and when occasion should arise, and if he does so with the intention of creating such a disposition in his hearers or readers, he will be guilty of the offence of attempting to excite disaffection within the meaning of the section, though no disturbance

is brought about by his words or any feeling of disaffection, in fact, produced by them. *It is sufficient for the purposes of the section that the words used are calculated to excite feelings of ill-will against the Government and to hold it up to the hatred and contempt of the people, and that they were used with the intention to create such feeling.* (Emphasis added)

He went on to distinguish between the British government and the administration to which powers were delegated by the government. He asserted that there was a great difference between dealing with government in that sense and dealing with any particular administration which exercised powers delegated to it. He asked, 'Were these articles intended to excite feelings of enmity against the Government, or, on the other hand, were they merely expressing, though in strong language, disapprobation of certain Government measures?' The jury was advised to bear in mind that the question they had to decide was whether the articles were published with the intention to commit the offence of sedition or not.

Upon considering the charge and the summation, the jury informed the court that it was unable to return a unanimous verdict. Justice Petheram would accept nothing less than a unanimous verdict and declared that a retrial before a different jury would be held at a future date. The retrial never took place because the accused issued an apology for the articles, due to which the prosecution was terminated.

Though the end was anticlimactic, the charge to the jury established the difference between disapprobation and disaffection, and echoed Justice Fitzgerald[20] in distinguishing between the government and its administrative delegates. This would have a bearing on the second trial for sedition, which is probably one of the most famous trials in Indian history and took place six years after the first.

The protagonist of this episode is Bal Gangadhar Tilak, one of the tallest personalities in modern Indian history. He was born in Ratnagiri[21] in the Bombay Presidency in 1856 and was home-schooled by his father, an academician, till the age of eleven. He commenced formal education at Poona High School, from where he matriculated in 1872. He was orphaned just before matriculation on the death of his father; his mother had passed away when he was ten. However, this did not deter him from higher studies and he graduated from Deccan College in Poona in 1876 with a Bachelor of Arts degree. He read law at Bombay University after graduation and obtained an LLB degree in 1879. Three events which occurred during his time at Bombay University shaped his nationalist ideology.[22]

The first was the trial and deposition of Malhar Rao Gaekwad, the maharaja of Baroda, by the British government in 1875 on the charges of poisoning the British Resident,[23] though this was not proved. The second event was an unsuccessful and minor uprising against the British in some parts of Maharashtra in 1876 which was allegedly led by one Vasudev Balwant Phadke. Though the uprising was quickly quelled, it left a deep impression on Tilak's mind. This impression was not one of approval, but he realized that any uprising has to be on the same level as that of the British—through superior education and organization. The third and most tragic event was the great Madras famine of 1877–78[24] caused due to drought and failure of crops in the Deccan, taking the lives of about 5.25 million people in the British Indian territories alone.[25] The famine, which spread to parts of Punjab, the North-West Frontier Province and the Central and United Provinces in the second year, was made worse by the export of crops by the British during the drought which made food grains scarce for the native population and caused deaths due to starvation and malnutrition.[26]

Tilak started two weekly periodicals in 1881: *Kesari*,[27] a Marathi vernacular, and *Mahratta*[28] which was published in English. His first brush with the law occurred in 1882 when he was imprisoned for four months, along with Gopal Ganesh Agarkar, the editor of *Kesari* and *Mahratta*. He was convicted for publishing purportedly defamatory articles against the native administrator of Kolhapur, alleging that he planned to poison the prince of Kolhapur. However, this only made Tilak more popular with the people, and he was given a reception befitting a hero when he was released from prison. Agarkar soon thereafter devoted himself to education and social reform. Tilak, having established the Deccan Education Society in 1880, joined the Indian National Congress in 1889.

Bal Gangadhar Tilak, like *Bangobasi* and many other orthodox Hindu public intellectuals and leaders, was opposed to the Age of Consent Bill. However, his opposition stood on a different footing than the other orthodox leaders. He believed that a foreign bureaucracy should not pass judgment on Hindu traditions and customs through legislation. He believed that instead of legislation the evil of intercourse with girl brides could be tackled through education. However, he went a step ahead from merely opposing the Bill and proposed that rather than having a general legislation like the Age of Consent Bill, social reformer leaders should bind themselves to the pledge[29] that girls and boys should not be married until they attain the age of sixteen and twenty, respectively. The reformers, of course, refused to be bound to this pledge.[30]

On 7 August 1895, Bal Gangadhar Tilak was elected to the governor general's Legislative Council for two years and took the customary oath of allegiance to the British monarch. However, he did not look at his election as an impediment to his nationalistic work. He said, 'An additional membership is, as I view it, no sop or gag intended to stop honest and fair criticism. But if it is, I should certainly give it up rather than consent to draw over the gross negligence or the palpable errors of officials, however high they may be.'[31]

The years 1895 and 1896 had deficient rainfall, and the resultant drought caused another great famine in the United Provinces, Central Provinces, Bihar, Bombay, Bengal, Central India, Rajputana, Punjab and Hyderabad. The reported number of deaths in British territories was 7,50,000, but the numbers would have been much greater as the figures for the native princely states were not available.[32]

Though the British Crown and Parliament had vowed to ameliorate the condition of the natives affected by famines, the bureaucracy in India was apathetic towards the sufferings of the rural farmers and peasants. Bal Gangadhar Tilak sent out volunteers across the regions in question and discovered that the number of people affected by the famine was far greater than that reported by the local revenue officers and bureaucrats. Tilak's volunteers apprised the affected population of their right to claim relief from the government and to seek concession from revenue collection. They encouraged them to not pay taxes at the cost of their lives and properties during the famine. *Kesari* did its part by dedicating its columns to speak out against the bureaucracy and suggested ways to ameliorate the conditions of the victims of the famine. These activities made Tilak very unpopular with the bureaucracy and the British government in India.[33]

The drought ended in 1897 on the back of a good monsoon but the sufferings did not end. Post-monsoon, a large number of people became victims of fever as well as a plague caused by rats. The fatalities caused by the disease were estimated to be about 10 million. In the aftermath of the outbreak, the British government took strict measures to arrest the spread of the disease but failed to seek public support. Tilak supported the efforts by starting a Plague Hospital in Poona and acted as a conduit between the people and the government. The government established a body called the Plague Committee comprised entirely of Europeans, headed by one Mr Rand. The committee used British soldiers to conduct house-to-house searches for patients who were sent to government hospitals, while the other members of the households were segregated from the populace. Their belongings were destroyed for fear of the infection spreading and their houses were left unguarded. While supporting the measures taken by the government, Tilak suggested various measures to make the activities popular and proposed that the patients could be sent to his hospital instead to ensure popular cooperation. However, the government did not pay heed and the Plague Committee carried on its efforts without taking cognizance of native sensitivities. As a result, Mr Rand and a British army officer accompanying him were assassinated by Damodar Chapekar, a militant nationalist, on 22 June 1897. The assassinations spread panic among the Anglo-Indian community and provided the government an excuse to mount a campaign of repression against the vernacular press.[34]

Earlier, an article in *Kesari* published on 23 April 1895 had reinvigorated the memory of Shivaji Maharaj in the mind of the public and sparked a campaign to renovate his tomb, which was situated within the Raigad fort in Maharashtra where he lived at the time of his death. In 1896, a festival was started to celebrate Shivaji Maharaj's birth anniversary on 19 February. The festival could not be held on his birth anniversary in 1897 due to the plague and it was decided that it would be held on the anniversary of his coronation which fell on 13 June. The festival was held over 12–13 June and was marked by speeches, prayers, hymn singing and reading of religious texts.[35]

15 June was marked by the publication of an article in *Kesari* reporting speeches delivered at the festival which justified and defended Shivaji Maharaj for killing Afzal Khan,[36] an act which was described as 'murder' by British historians. The speech had disapproved of this label and asserted that the killing was an act of defence and Shivaji Maharaj was justified in his act as he believed he was under attack. The article quoted a speaker as saying, 'Every Hindu, every Maratha, to whatever party he may belong, must rejoice at this [Shivaji] festival. We all are striving to regain [our] lost independence, and this terrible load is to be uplifted by us all in combination. It will never be proper to place obstacles in the way of any person who, with a true mind, follows the path of uplifting this burden in the manner he deems fit. . . . If any one be crushing down the country from above, cut him off; but do not put impediments in the way of others.' Another speaker was quoted as saying, 'If no one blames Napoleon for committing two thousand murders in Europe, [and] if Caesar is considered merciful though he needlessly committed slaughters in Gaul [France] many a time, why should so virulent an attack be made on Shri Shivaji Maharaja for killing one or two persons? The people who took part in the French Revolution denied that they committed murders and maintained that they were [only] removing thorns from (their). Why should not the same principle [argument] be made applicable to Maharashtra?'

Thereafter, Tilak himself was reported to have delivered a speech justifying the killing of Afzal Khan, reportedly saying, 'Did Shivaji commit a sin in killing Afzulkhan or how? The answer to this question can be found in the

Mahabharat itself. Shrimat Krishna's advice [teaching] in the Gita is to kill even our teachers [and] our kinsmen. No blame attaches [to any person] if [he] is doing deeds without being actuated by a desire to reap the fruit [of his deeds]. Shri Shivaji Maharaj did nothing with a view to fill in the small void of his own stomach [from interested motives]. With benevolent intentions he murdered Afzulkhan for the good of others. If thieves enter our house and we have not (sufficient) strength in our wrists to drive them out, we should without hesitation shut them up and burn them alive. God has not conferred upon the Mlenchhas[37] the grant inscribed on a copperplate of the kingdom of Hindustan. The Maharaja strove to drive them away from the land of his birth; he did not thereby commit the sin of coveting what belonged to others. Do not circumscribe your vision like a frog in a well. Get out of the Penal Code, enter into the high atmosphere of the Shrimat Bhagwatgita, and [then] consider the actions of great men.'[38]

Anglo-Indian press like the *Times of India* blamed Tilak and *Kesari* for the assassination of Mr Rand as it occurred immediately after the publication of the above article. Such imputations were made even though there was no apparent link between the articles and the murder. The *Times of India* openly suggested that Tilak was guilty of sedition. To counter the Anglo-Indian narrative, Tilak started publishing a series of articles in *Kesari* from 20 July 1897 to explain what sedition meant. He went to Bombay from Poona on 27 July to seek legal recourse against the *Times of India*.[39]

Meanwhile, on 26 July, the Bombay government directed Mirza Abbas Ali Baig, the Oriental translator to the government, to file a complaint under Section 124A against Tilak in his capacity as publisher, proprietor and editor of *Kesari,* and against Hari Narayan Gokhale, the printer of the newspaper. The complaint was filed before the chief presidency magistrate of Bombay on 27 July and Tilak was arrested late at night even though the government was aware that he was in Bombay throughout the day. Unsuccessful bail pleas on behalf of Tilak were rejected on 28 July by the magistrate and on 29 July by the Bombay High Court. However, when his trial was committed to the Bombay High Court on 2 August, another bail plea filed on the same day was allowed by Justice Badruddin Tyabji.[40]

A word on the characters at this stage. Justice Tyabji was the first Indian barrister to practise before the Bombay High Court. He was a founding member of the Indian National Congress, and he presided over its 1887 session, making him the first Muslim person to do so. Interestingly, the judge who denied bail to Tilak was none other than Justice Mahadev Govind Ranade, the founder of the Industrial Association of Western India and another founding member of the Indian National Congress![41]

The lawyer who represented Tilak before the magistrate and the High Court in his bail proceedings was Sir Dinshaw Davar, who was later appointed as a judge of the Bombay High Court in 1908. He eventually became its acting chief justice in 1914.

After being enlarged on bail, Tilak was under great financial strain. However, he was bolstered by the help of friends and supporters who raised a public fund to help him prepare for his defence, for which supporters from even as far as Bengal sent contributions. The trial for sedition was scheduled for 8 September 1897 but no Bombay-based barrister was willing to take up the defence for Tilak. Rabindranath Tagore was forced to intervene and helped Tilak engage Mr Pugh and Mr Garth, two Calcutta-based English barristers, to appear for his defence before the High Court. The prosecutor on behalf of the government was Mr Basil Lang, the advocate general. The trial was presided over by Justice Arthur Strachey and was heard by a jury of nine members, out of which six were European and thus unacquainted with Marathi, the language in which the articles were published.[42]

The advocate general opened the case by reading Section 124A of the IPC. He referred to the word 'disaffection' in Section 124A to have the same meaning as defined by Johnson's Dictionary and Webster's Dictionary, among others, and referred to the *Bangobasi* case where the term was defined by Justice Petheram in his charge to the jury. He laid out the government's case before the jury by stating:

> It is not necessary to prove that the writings in the *Kesari*, whether poetical or otherwise, incited a particular person to commit a violent act or create sedition in his mind. It is enough if there is only a possibility of it. If a particular piece of writing is calculated to create in the reader's mind a desire to try overthrow of Government, it should fall under the category of sedition. Tilak is an honourable gentleman, a fellow of the Senate of the Bombay University and a Member of the Legislative Council. The circulation of the *Kesari* is about 7,000 copies, about a thousand of which are distributed in Bombay. The paper is a weighty and influential journal and calculated to mould the reader's mind. It describes the Government as foreign. It asserts that the people are being crushed under tyranny. The Shivaji festival may be unexceptional in itself, but it has been given a political colour and has been used as an instrument to create a feeling of disaffection against the Government. The court has to consider the total effect of the articles and not isolated words or passages. It is one thing to say that India

is suffering from poverty and another to connect that statement with the story of Shivaji and Afzal Khan. The whole aspect [of] it is changed. The duty of remaining discontented in order to flourish has been preached by the accused without any disguise. All writings of the accused tend towards creation of a feeling of resentment against the powers that be.

Lang further contended that it was significant that the two murders happened within a week of the publication of the articles in *Kesari*, despite having no evidence to substantiate this imputation.

Pugh, in defence of Tilak, submitted that the articles on the basis of which Tilak was charged did not fall within Section 124A. He stated that Tilak had taken an independent line with regard to the measures against the plague and had in fact cooperated with the government in ameliorating the condition of the victims. He contended that the articles were in fact in furtherance of loyalty to the government even though they set forth certain grievances, which could not be called seditious. He contended that there was no suggestion of overthrowing the British government, as such action could only be brought about by Hindus and Muslims uniting, which was something that praise of Shivaji Maharaj could not have brought about. He referred to James F. Stephen's speech in the Legislative Council delivered while introducing Section 124A to contend that the dictionary meaning of the word 'disaffection' had to be ignored in favour of a legal meaning. He contended that 'disaffection' under Section 124A could only refer to the creation of a rebellious spirit against the government. In his statement to the jury, he said:

But for the murder of Rand, Tilak would never have been hauled up in court. Most of the subject-matter of Tilak's alleged offences is in the form of verses. A metrical composition does not lend itself to a strictly legal, precise and scientific analysis. The Shivaji festival is very much like the festival of Robert Bruce and William Wallace. When people are fired with enthusiasm for such national festivities, they do use some extravagant, hyperbolic and metaphorical language. The controversy about Afzal Khan's murder was in the Press long before Rand's murder, and by no stretch of the imagination could that murder be related to the murder of Afzal Khan. If the Government seriously believed Tilak guilty of the abetment of murder, it ought to have openly accused him of it. The very fact that he has not been so charged but prosecuted under 124A, shows the weakness [of the] Government's case. . . . Sedition whether in England or in India, must have the same connotation. A spicy description of a thousand and one grievances of the people, even when enumerated for the purpose of creating discontent among them must not be condemned as sedition. An isolated murder like that of Rand would neither ruin nor shake the foundations of the British Empire. Tilak's articles written in connection with the Diamond Jubilee of Queen Victoria constituted sufficient proof of his loyalty to the Crown as of his genuine patriotism.

After hearing the advocate general and Pugh, Justice Strachey proceeded to deliver his charge to the jury on the fifth day of the trial. He summed up by saying:

You will thus see that the whole question is one of the intention of the accused in publishing these articles. Did they intend to excite in the minds of their readers feelings of disaffection or enmity to the Government? Or did they intend merely to excite disapprobation of certain Government measures? Or did they intend to excite no feeling adverse either to the Government or its measures, but only to excite interest in a poem about Shivaji and a historical discussion about his alleged killing of a Mahomedan General?[43]

Justice Strachey then discussed the articles in detail and suggested that the case be looked at under two issues. He said:

First of all, you must remember the test to be applied is whether these people were trying to stir up a rebellion or feeling of enmity against the Government. Secondly, it is for you to consider the class of readers of the publication and the state of feelings at the time the articles were published, and the natural effect which according to their view the articles of the 15th of June would have upon them at such a time.

However, he further restricted the first issue by telling the jury:

You are to read the articles with the other evidence and, putting aside all prejudice, say if Tilak was trying to make his readers hate the Government, or was commenting on measures with a view to excite disapprobation compatible with a definite policy to support the Government.

He followed the definition of 'disaffection' as laid down by Justice Petheram in his charge to the jury in the *Bangobasi* case, which has been discussed earlier in this chapter. Justice Strachey gave a very wide meaning to the word to the extent that 'disaffection' would mean a mere lack of affection, and a feeling which did not translate into an overt act of hatred, enmity, dislike, hostility, contempt, or any other form of ill will against the government. He opined that 'disloyalty' was perhaps the best term to describe 'disaffection' as it comprehended every possible form of bad feeling for the government. He said:

> That is what the law means by the disaffection which a man must not excite or attempt to excite; he must not make or try to make others feel enmity of any kind towards the Government . . . if a man excites or attempts to excite feelings of disaffection, great or small, he is guilty under the section.

He further directed the jury to understand the term 'government' to mean 'the British rule or its representatives as such—the existing political system as distinguished from any particular set of administrators'.

In directing the jury as to the meaning of the Explanation in Section 124A, Justice Strachey said:

> . . . while the first clause shows affirmatively what the offence made punishable by the section is, the explanation states negatively what it is not. It says that something 'is not disaffection' and 'is not an offence within this clause'. Therefore its object is to protect from the condemnation pronounced by the first clause certain acts which it distinguishes from the disloyal attempts which the first clause

deals with. The next and most important point for you to bear in mind is that the thing protected by the explanation is 'the making of comments on the measures of the Government with a certain intention'. This shows that the explanation has a strictly defined and limited scope. Observe that it has no application whatever unless you come to the conclusion that the writings in question can fairly and reasonably be construed as 'the making of comments on the measures of the Government'. It does not apply to any other writings except that.

Thus, he further restricted the scope of inquiry by the jury by directing that the Explanation to Section 124A only applied to writings which consisted of mere criticism of specific measures or actions of the government like an enactment, tax or social schemes, and not to any writings which went beyond such criticism and incited or attempted to incite disaffection against the government. He relied on the explanation provided by Justice Petheram in the *Bangobasi* case to distinguish between 'disaffection' and 'disapprobation' and added that this distinction is the 'essence of the section'.

While the jury deliberated on the case against Tilak, Pugh requested the court to reserve the question on the definition of 'disaffection' irrespective of the outcome of the trial. There were other sedition trials pending at that point of time and Pugh did not want the decision in the Tilak case to have a bearing on and prejudicing the other trials by definitively ruling on the meaning of 'disaffection'. Reserving the question would have ensured that the other courts would have been free to interpret 'disaffection' in the manner it was intended to have meant when James F. Stephen proposed the introduction of Section 124A in the IPC. Justice Strachey, however, refused to reserve this question and decided that the definition as expounded in his charge to the jury was fair and balanced.

On the seventh day, the jury found in favour of the prosecution and convicted Tilak for the offence of sedition under Section 124A by a majority of six to three. He was sentenced to rigorous imprisonment for a term of eighteen months by the court.

The defence immediately applied for permission for leave to appeal the verdict mainly on the grounds that the definitions of 'disaffection' and 'government' as laid down by Justice Strachey were incorrect. The application was heard on 24 September 1897 and rejected by a special bench comprising of Chief Justice Charles F. Farran, Justice E.T. Candy and Justice Strachey.

Upon the High Court's refusal to grant the certificate of leave to appeal to the Privy Council in England, which exercised the power of sitting in appeal over the Indian High Courts, Tilak filed a petition in the Privy Council seeking leave to appeal against the verdict of the Bombay High Court. The petition was filed mainly on the ground that the meaning of 'disaffection' as laid down by Justice Strachey was incorrect. Tilak was represented by H.H. Asquith, QC, who later served as the prime minister of England from 1908 to 1916. He contended that Tilak's comments had not exceeded what in England would be considered within the meaning of public journalism. He emphasized that the misdirection by incorrectly defining 'disaffection' would not only affect Tilak but also the entire Indian press and Indian subjects of the British Crown. He argued that the definition adversely affected the liberty of press, the right to free speech and public meeting, and the right to petition for redressal of grievances. It was further contended that the right direction would have been that an essential ingredient of the offence of sedition under Section 124A would be such a state of enmity as would be incompatible with a disposition to obey the government.[44]

After hearing the arguments for and against granting leave to appeal to the Queen in Council, the Privy Council decided that it was not a fit case for grant of such leave as no case had been made out by Tilak to entitle him to leave to appeal. The dismissal of the petition on 19 November 1897 concluded the appeals process and Tilak was consigned to suffer rigorous imprisonment.

He was initially imprisoned in the Dongri and Byculla jails in Bombay but was subsequently transferred to Yerawada jail in Poona. His health suffered greatly while he was in prison, and a person of his stature and intellect being imprisoned like a hardened criminal caused a major outrage. The British government was petitioned by Professor Max Mueller, Sir William Hunter, Sir Richard Garth, William Caine, Dadabhai Naoroji, Romesh Chandra Dutt and some members of the British Parliament seeking an early release for Tilak. The British government sought to impose the condition that he would give up politics if he was released early, a condition that was rejected outright. Another condition was that he would accept public receptions or felicitations upon his release, which Tilak readily accepted. He was also told that if he was found guilty of sedition again, he would be sentenced with an additional period of six months, which was the remainder of his term of sentence. Upon acceptance of these conditions, Bal Gangadhar Tilak was released from prison on 3 September 1898 at 10.30 p.m. after serving fifty-one weeks of his sentence.[45]

At the time Tilak's trial was going on before the Bombay High Court, another trial for sedition under Section 124A was under way before the Sessions Court[46] of Satara, a district in present-day western Maharashtra.[47] A vernacular by the name of *Pratod*[48] published at Islampur in Satara district was prosecuted for sedition for publishing an article titled 'Preparations for Becoming Independent' on 17 May 1897 which stated:[49]

> Canada is a country in North America under the British rule, the people of which have now become intolerant of their subjection to England. Though they are subject to the British people, they are not effeminate like the people of India. It is not their hard lot to starve themselves for filling the purse of Englishmen. They are not obliged to pay a pie to England. Their income from land-revenue and taxes are expended for their own benefit. They enact their own laws independently, and appoint their own officers, except one or two who are sent from England. Of even this nominal dependence they have become impatient, and are now busy making efforts to throw it off. It is natural for them to envy their neighbours, who after casting off their English nationality, and assuming the designation of Americans, are now enjoying the blessings of a free nation. They have appointed a committee to frame an independent constitution for themselves. This committee has issued a notification of their aims, copies of which have been distributed even in India. In this notification they have clearly stated their intention of throwing off the English yoke, and establishing a Government of their own. Like us, they are not men given to prattling, but can act up to their word. There is also strong unity amongst them. Spirited men show by their actions what stuff they are made of. There are no people on earth who are so effeminate and helpless as those of India. We have become so callous and shameless that we do

not feel humiliation, while we are laughed at by all
nations for losing such a vast and gold-like country
as India. What manliness we can exhibit in such a
condition is self-evident.

The Sessions Court found the publisher and proprietor of
Pratod guilty of sedition under Section 124A and sentenced
them to transportation for life and seven years' rigorous
imprisonment, respectively. The accused filed an appeal[50]
before the Bombay High Court which was heard by a full
bench of the High Court comprising Chief Justice Charles
F. Farran, Justice H.J. Parsons and Justice Mahadeo Govind
Ranade. The High Court upheld the guilty verdict passed
by the Sessions Court and found that the article was based
on false assertions and misreported the aspirations of the
Canadian subjects of the British Crown. In doing so, the
court found that the article provoked and instigated its
readers by calling them effeminate and asking them to be
strong-spirited men. Therefore, Chief Justice Farran held
that the accused were guilty of exciting disaffection against
the government established by law in British India. Justice
Parsons concurred with the chief justice and found that
the article attempted to excite its readers to overthrow the
British government and replace it with another government.
Justice Ranade also agreed with his fellow judges and found
that the article intended to excite feelings of aversion and
hatred against the British government. He further held that
it attempted to use an 'imaginary ideal of independence'
and tried to instigate its readers to imitate that ideal against
the British government in India. He held that the article
would be covered by the provisions of Section 124A and
thus punishable for sedition. Justice Ranade's definition of
'disaffection' is to be noted. He said:

> Disaffection, as thus judicially paraphrased, is a positive political distemper and not a mere absence or negation of love or good-will. It is a positive feeling of aversion which is akin to 'disloyalty', a defiant insubordination of authority, or when it is not defiant, it secretly seeks to alienate the people, and weaken the bond of allegiance, and prepossesses the minds of the people with avowed or secret animosity to Government, a feeling which tends to bring the Government into hatred or contempt by imputing base or corrupt motives to it, makes men indisposed to obey or support the laws of the realm, and promotes discontent and public disorder.[51]

Justice Ranade's exposition of 'disaffection' was at odds with Justice Strachey's exposition in Tilak's case and appeared to be the more accurate of the two expositions. Being restrictive in nature, Justice Ranade's exposition was representative of what James F. Stephen intended to include within Section 124A of the IPC, which was that mere thoughts or state of mind cannot be considered sedition. The case ended on 24 November 1897 with the High Court upholding the conviction, but the sentences were considerably reduced for being disproportionate. The editor was sentenced to one year of rigorous imprisonment, and the proprietor to three months' simple imprisonment.

The year 1897 was rounded off by the third sedition verdict of the year in the case of *Queen Empress v. Amba Prasad*[52] which was decided on 14 December 1897 by a full bench[53] of the Allahabad High Court comprising Chief Justice John Edge, Justice Harrison Falkner Blair and Justice William Robert Burkitt. The court was hearing an appeal arising out of a conviction for sedition by the Sessions Court at Moradabad[54] pertaining to an article published on 14 July

1897 by one Amba Prasad, who was the proprietor, editor and publisher of a vernacular newspaper named *Jami-ul-Ulam*. The article was titled 'Azadi band hone se kabal namuna'.[55] Amba Prasad was quick to plead guilty, and on being asked to show cause why he should not be punished he said, 'I can give no reason. Through inexperience I have committed this fault, for which I am very ashamed, and I wish to throw myself unconditionally upon the mercy of the Government. This is all I wish to say.' The Sessions Court accordingly held him guilty of sedition under Section 124A and sentenced him to eighteen months' rigorous imprisonment.

Finding the sentence too severe and harsh, Amba Prasad appealed before the Allahabad High Court and argued that the Sessions Court should have taken his unconditional apology into consideration. He also compared his case with Tilak's case and contended that his offence was much milder as compared to Tilak's but the sentence was still the same, and therefore asked for a lesser nominal penalty in this context.

The High Court deemed it fit to look at past cases to determine the degree of offence and whether the milder nature of the offence would entitle Amba Prasad to a lighter sentence. Thus, it looked at the *Bangobasi* case, Tilak's case and the *Pratod* case and reached the conclusion that the difficulty in determining the true meaning of Section 124A was caused by the explanation to the section. The judges relied heavily on the charge to the jury by Justice Strachey in Tilak's case, which in turn had relied on the *Bangobasi* case. In relying on the *Pratod* case the judges found the reports of the case, as far as the opinions of Justice Parsons and Justice Ranade were concerned, to be too imperfect to be relied upon. Seems convenient when you look at it now, considering Justice Ranade had probably provided the most accurate exposition of the law at that time. The judges merely assumed that if their opinions differed from Justice Strachey's exposition then the Privy Council would most probably not approve of the same having approved Justice Strachey's exposition in Tilak's case.

After looking at the facts of the case, the court reached the conclusion that Amba Prasad had attempted to excite active disloyalty and rebellion amongst the Mohammedan subjects of the British government in India, as the newspaper in question enjoyed a largely Mohammedan readership. Having found so, the High Court held that he did not deserve any reduction of sentence and dismissed his appeal.

Soon thereafter, on 25 December 1897, a Bill to amend Section 124A was introduced in the governor general's Legislative Council considering the events of 1897. The Council was of the view that the law which existed then was not drafted clearly by James F. Stephen. It felt that the judgments by the Calcutta, Bombay and Allahabad High Courts interpreted Section 124A in accordance with English law, so it would only be appropriate to amend the section to bring it explicitly in accordance with English law. The Bill therefore sought to repeal Section 124A and proposed to replace it with a new Section 124A which would read as:[56]

> Whoever by words, either spoken or written, or by signs, or by visible representation, or otherwise, brings or attempts to bring into hatred or contempt, or excites or attempts to excite disaffection towards Her Majesty or the Government, or promotes or attempts to promote feelings of enmity or ill-will between different classes of Her Majesty's subjects shall be punished with transportation for life or any shorter term to which fine may be added, or with

imprisonment which may extend to ten years, to which fine may be added, or with fine.

Explanation 1.—The expression 'disaffection' includes disloyalty and all feelings of enmity or ill-will.

Explanation 2.—Comments on the measures of the Government with a view to obtain their alteration by lawful means, without exciting or attempting to excite hatred, contempt or disaffection do not constitute an offence.

The Bill underwent further revision on 18 February 1898 by the removal of 'or promotes or attempts to promote feelings of enmity or ill-will between different classes of Her Majesty's subjects' from the principal section, and the term 'ill-will' from Explanation 1. The term 'Government' was replaced by 'Government established by law in British India', and another explanation was added to protect the fair criticism of government measures which did not necessarily seek reforms as provided under Explanation 2. Section 124A was revised as follows (the italicized words are the additions):[57]

Whoever by words, either spoken or written, or by signs, or by visible representation, or otherwise, brings or attempts to bring into hatred or contempt, or excites or attempts to excite disaffection towards Her Majesty or the Government *established by law in British India*, ~~or promotes or attempts to promote feelings of enmity or ill-will between different classes of Her Majesty's subjects~~ shall be punished with transportation for life or any shorter term to which fine may be added, or with imprisonment which may extend to ~~ten~~ *three* years, to which fine may be added, or with fine.

Explanation 1.—The expression 'disaffection' includes disloyalty and all feelings of enmity ~~or ill-will~~.

Explanation 2.—Comments *expressing disapprobation of* ~~on~~ the measures of the Government with a view to obtain their alteration by lawful means, without exciting or attempting to excite hatred, contempt or disaffection do not constitute an offence *under this section*.

Explanation 3.—Comments expressing disapprobation of the administrative or other action of the Government without exciting or attempting to excite hatred, contempt or disaffection, do not constitute an offence under this section.

Clearly, Justice Petheram's and Justice Strachey's charge to the jury, in the *Bangobasi* case and the Tilak case respectively, prevailed upon the Legislative Council which explicitly defined 'disaffection' in line with their exposition and made it wider than the offence under English law, contrary to what was intended by James F. Stephen. Explanations 2 and 3 were added as a positive assertion of the principle that people were at liberty to criticize the actions and conduct of the government and the bureaucracy—including demanding rollbacks or reforms—by lawful means.

Sir Alexander Mackenzie, then lieutenant governor of Bengal, explained that the necessity of the revision stemmed from the fact that ever since the Vernacular Press Act had been repealed in 1881, the vernacular Indian press had grown more adversarial and defiant of the British government. He felt that the growth of such writing would eventually result in the collapse of law and order and active resistance against the British government. He even blamed English education for the rise of unemployed but educated youth who turned to writing such articles in the vernacular press out of discontent.[58]

Therefore, upon revision of the proposed provision, the new Section 124A as enacted by Act IV of 1898 read as under:

> Whoever by words, either spoken or written, or by signs, or by visible representation, or otherwise, brings or attempts to bring into hatred or contempt, or excites or attempts to excite disaffection towards Her Majesty or the Government established by law in British India, shall be punished with transportation for life or any shorter term to which fine may be added, or with imprisonment which may extend to three years, to which fine may be added, or with fine.
>
> Explanation 1.—The expression 'disaffection' includes disloyalty and all feelings of enmity.
>
> Explanation 2.—Comments expressing disapprobation of the measures of the Government with a view to obtain their alteration by lawful means, without exciting or attempting to excite hatred, contempt or disaffection do not constitute an offence under this section.
>
> Explanation 3.—Comments expressing disapprobation of the administrative or other action of the Government without exciting or attempting to excite hatred, contempt or disaffection, do not constitute an offence under this section.

The deletions from the proposed Section 124A were separately enacted as a new provision, Section 153A of the IPC, which punished the promotion of enmity between classes, or class hatred. The new Section 153A as enacted in 1898 read as under:[59]

Whoever by words, either spoken or written, or by signs, or by visible representation, or otherwise, promotes or attempts to promote feelings of enmity or hatred between different classes of Her Majesty's subjects shall be punished with imprisonment which may extend to two years, or with fine, or with both.

Explanation.—It does not amount to an offence with the meaning of this section to point out, without malicious intention and with an honest view to their removal, matters which are producing, or have a tendency to produce, feelings of enmity or hatred between different classes of Her Majesty's subjects.

The removal and separate enactment of this provision was necessary because retention of the provision would have expanded the scope of Section 124A to also cover promotion of class hatred, which was never the intention of the Legislative Council. Therefore, Section 153A was inserted under the category of offences against public tranquillity and not as an offence against the State.

Another provision which was recast and enacted by the same Act IV of 1898 was Section 505 of the IPC which penalized statements conducing to public mischief. Even though it was under the chapter of offences of criminal intimidation, insult and annoyance, it was closer to Sections 124A and 153A in its application. Section 505 as enacted in 1898 read as under:[60]

Whoever makes, publishes or circulates any statement, rumour or report,

(a) with intent to cause, or which is likely to cause, any officer, soldier or sailor in the Royal Indian Marine or in the Imperial

Service Troops to mutiny or otherwise disregard or fail in his duty as such; or

(b) with intent to cause, or which is likely to cause, fear or alarm to the public, whereby any person may be induced to commit an offence against the State or against the public tranquillity; or

(c) with intent to incite, or which is likely to incite, any class or community of persons to commit any offence against any other class or community;

shall be punished with imprisonment which may extend to two years, or with fine, or with both.

Exception. It does not amount to an offence, within the meaning of this section, when the person making, publishing or circulating any such statement, rumour or report has reasonable grounds for believing that such statement, rumour or report is true, and makes, publishes or circulates it without any such intent as aforesaid.

The exception to Section 505 distinguished it from Section 124A as the latter did not carve out an exception for writings or words which may be true. In other words, there was no defence of truth available under Section 124A as long as the writings or words excited disaffection against the British government.

5

Revolutionary Sedition

The turn of the century saw the beginning of a new chapter in Indian nationalism, considering the British government, more or less, had had a peaceful existence after the mutiny of 1857. It also saw a change in guard at the helm of the British Empire with the death of Queen Victoria on 22 January 1901 and the consequent ascension of King Edward VII to the throne as the emperor of India. Victoria had ascended to the throne of the United Kingdom of Great Britain and Ireland as an eighteen-year-old in 1837 and was officially proclaimed as the empress of India on 1 May 1876. She considered India as the crown jewel of the British Empire even though she never once visited the country.[1]

Globally, the advent of the twentieth century brought about major geopolitical changes. Queen Victoria's last years saw the South African Boer war (1899–1902) where the British army entered into conflict with the Boers, descendants of the settlers of the Dutch East India Company, for control of two Boer nations which were rich in gold and other precious minerals.[2]

Russia and Japan entered a war in 1904 over a fight for regional economic superiority. The war proved disastrous for

Russia, both on the battle fronts and at home. Public opinion against the war resulted in nationwide political campaigns opposing the repressive Russian autocracy headed by the tsar, who quickly lost the people's confidence. Things went out of control when the tsar used force to crush a peaceful peasants' march on 9 January 1905 in St Petersburg killing or injuring hundreds of its citizens. This incident, known as 'Bloody Sunday', sparked off a countrywide bloody revolution which caused the tsar to concede important civil liberties and legislative powers to the opposition.[3]

The Russian Revolution of 1905 sparked off political unrest across the East. Mass movements occurred in Persia in 1906, China in 1907 and the Ottoman Empire of Turkey in 1908.[4]

The most monumental event that occurred in the first decade of the twentieth century in India was the partition of Bengal in 1905, which changed the face of the Indian subcontinent forever; the ramifications of the action are being felt till date. Before partition, Bengal comprised forty-eight districts with an area of about 1,90,000 square miles. The population of Bengal was about 78 million and the region comprised of present-day Bengal, Bangladesh, Bihar, Orissa and Chota Nagpur (in Jharkhand).

On 7 July 1905, the British Viceroy Lord Curzon announced the decision to partition Bengal into two provinces of East Bengal and West Bengal. East Bengal was a Muslim-majority province which mainly comprised of parts of Assam, Chittagong and Dhaka (which became the capital) and the Rajasahi regions of Bengal. The British government justified the decision as an administrative necessity as Bengal was too large to be efficiently administered. When the proposal to partition Bengal was officially mooted by Lord Curzon in 1904 it was met with widespread opposition across the region as it was seen as an attempt to destroy Bengali as well as Hindu–Muslim unity and nationalism which was on the rise. Not just publications like the *Muslim Chronicle*[5] but even Anglo-Indian newspapers like the *Statesman*, *Englishman* and *Times of India* condemned the move. Interestingly, the move was also criticized by newspapers in England such as the *Times*, *Manchester Guardian* and *Daily News*.[6]

The suspicion that the reasons for the partition were more political than administrative was confirmed by Lord Curzon's letter of 17 February 1904 to the secretary of state for India where he wrote:

> The Bengalis, who like to think of themselves a nation, and who dream of a future when the English will have been turned out and Bengali Babu will be installed Government House, Calcutta, of course bitterly resent any disruption that will be likely to interfere with the realisation of this dream. If we are weak enough to yield to their clamour now, we shall not be able to dismember or reduce Bengal again; and you will be cementing and solidifying, on the eastern flanks of India, a force already formidable and certain to be a source of increasing trouble in future.

In another letter dated 22 February 1905 he wrote:

> Calcutta is the centre from which the Congress party is manipulated throughout the whole of Bengal, and indeed the whole of India. Its best wirepullers and its most frothy orators reside there. The perfection of their machinery, and the tyranny which it enables them to exercise, are truly remarkable. They dominate public opinion in Calcutta; they affect the

High Court; they frighten the Local Government
and they are sometimes not without serious
influence upon the Government of India. The whole
of their activity is directed to creating an agency so
powerful that they may one day be able to force a
weak Government to give them what they desire.

He created a wedge between the two religions predominant
in Bengal by claiming that he wanted to partition Bengal
to provide the Muslims of East Bengal a province and to
promote Muslim unity which he claimed they had not
enjoyed for ages.[7]

The move to partition Bengal was met with fierce
resistance across the country but the circumcentre of the
movement was in Calcutta and across Bengal, both East and
West. The government reacted by suppressing nationalist
feelings by banning the singing of patriotic songs and the
chanting of 'Bande Mataram'.[8] It hindered public meetings
with the use of force and was generous in prosecuting
students, including schoolboys. The British were successful
in winning over the Muslims of East Bengal and espoused
their cause of a separate province led by the nawab of Dhaka,
which led to large-scale communal riots in East Bengal.[9]

The Indian National Congress was openly opposed to
the partition since 1903, and Gopal Krishna Gokhale in his
presidential address in 1905 called it a 'cruel wrong'. The
Bengalis reacted to the partition by starting the Swadeshi
Movement whereby they boycotted all foreign and British
goods and products and championed the use of indigenous
goods and products. Tilak said, 'We must raise a nation
on this soil. Love of nation is one's first duty. Next comes
religion and the Government. Our duty to the nation will be
the first. Swadeshi and Swadeshi will be our cry forever and
by this we will grow in spite of the rulers.'[10] The Swadeshi

Movement crippled imports and hurt the British government financially.

From 1905 onwards, the Indian National Congress was divided into two groups: the moderates and the nationalists. The moderates were led by Gopal Krishna Gokhale and Phirozeshah Mehta and the nationalists by Bal Gangadhar Tilak and Lala Lajpat Rai. In 1906, the Indian National Congress session at Calcutta supported the Swadeshi Movement and called for Swaraj or 'self-rule' which, in the words of Dadabhai Naoroji, meant 'the absolute right of self-taxation, self-legislation and self-administration'.

A violent revolutionary movement in Bengal was promoted by a periodical called *Jugantar,* which meant 'new era'. It was founded in March 1906 by Barindra Kumar Ghose, Abinash Bhattacharya and Bhupendranath Dutt as a revolutionary weekly and was published in Bengali. It was used as a platform for propaganda by Bengali revolutionaries like Barindra Kumar Ghose and Jatin Banerjee. The periodical made no pretence and openly served the cause of overthrow of the British government. It suggested fighting the British through brute force and once wrote, 'In a country where the ruling power relies on brute force to oppress its subjects, it is impossible to bring about revolution or a change in rulers through moral strength. In such a situation, subjects too must rely on brute force.' In another article titled 'Sedition and the Foreign King' it questioned the legitimacy of the British rule as it was based on treachery and thus lacked legal and ethical basis. The government reacted by arresting Bhupendranath Dutt in July 1907 and charged him under Section 124A of the IPC. He was sentenced to one year's imprisonment on being found guilty of sedition.[11]

The trial, known as the *Jugantar* case, titled *Emperor v. Phanendra Nath Mitter*[12] took place in 1908 at the

Calcutta High Court. Mitter was accused of committing the offence of sedition for the publication of three articles in Bengali in *Jugantar*. The first article 'Death Wished For' said:

> The extensive undertaking which we have begun for making our country independent. The hand of him who shrinks from uselessly shedding blood will tremble at the time of usefully shedding blood . . . So long as we shall not be fit for entering into this field of devotion, so long shall we have to practise useless shedding of blood, so long the play of this sort of fruitless death will have to be played . . . But the restless youth, who has for many days wandered about restless, aiming at the life of the enemy of his country with the object of removing him altogether, the hopeless fellow who has run into the jaws of death as the result of failure, why do not the tears of sympathy of the people of the country keep his memory alive? Why does his conduct get soiled by the stigma of rebellion? If self-destroyer and self-offeror be the epithets applied to rebels and heroes, respectively, where then lies the difference between them? . . . Whom have we placed in the van of the preparations for an expedition against the ruling power, which we have recently made? . . . A call to death is now being sounded. Let nobody remain indifferent any longer, let those who know how to die lead the van in this party of pilgrims. So long as the preparations for the work of war are not complete, so long will you have to die in vain. There is no help for it, even the shaft levelled at the foe hurts the breast of the innocent.[13]

The second article, title not mentioned in the judgment, said:

> These untold self-sacrificing, firmly resolute, heroic, self-restrained young men afraid of dharma, who in the opening days of the year 1315, having staked their lives in an attempt to remove the sorrows and the unhappy lot of the country, have to-day fallen into the grasp of the firingee, through the efforts of the traitor, have been born again and again in order to establish the kingdom of righteousness in India . . . The rod of providence has been uplifted in order to destroy the Mlechchha kingdom.

The final article, titled 'Conspiracy or Desire for Freedom', said:

> 'The word conspiracy is very ugly, and implies meanness. It is only a secret plot against the King which is called conspiracy. Did the prisoners in Calcutta get up a plot against the King in secret? Surely not. A secret effort or endeavour for gaining independence cannot be called a conspiracy. And the English, again, are not the rulers of this country. Nobody can take as a conspiracy the attempt or expedition against one who is not the king, but a robber, a thief, a barbarian, an uncivilised person, and an enemy of India.

The court referred to a few other articles which were not the subject of the charge of sedition but were used to demonstrate intention. Based on the three articles which were the subject of the charge under Section 124A, the jury found Mitter guilty of sedition.[14]

Jugantar was unable to survive the spate of sedition prosecutions and the consequent financial crisis and wound up operations in 1908.[15]

The anti-partition Swadeshi and Swaraj Movements spread to the Madras Presidency where in September 1907 a British police inspector named Bell was murdered by a constable, who immediately committed suicide. His funeral became a platform for anti-European and anti-British demonstrations. One Chidambaram Pillai delivered subversive speeches at Tuticorin and Tinnevelly[16] in February and March 1908. In a speech delivered on 9 March 1908, he said:

> As soon as the English people set foot in India, poverty also made its appearance in the country. So long as the foreign Government exists we shall not prosper. So long as we continue to be the servants and slaves of foreigners we shall have to endure hardships. Three-fourths of the Englishmen now in India are traders. If we all unite and make up our minds not to purchase their goods what business will they have here? They must all run back to their country. Besides, if we avoid going to these accursed Civil, Criminal and Police Courts, the remaining fourth of the English will have no work to do. Thus all the white men will run away from our country. Being thirty-three crores of people how astonishing it is that we are slaves to three crores. The cause of our growing poorer day by day is that one hundred and eighty crores of rupees are carried away each year in steam ships to a country six thousand miles away. What country can stand such treatment as this?[17]

Chidambaram Pillai was prosecuted for sedition under Section 124A, and for disturbing public tranquillity under Section 153A of the IPC for delivering this speech. He was sentenced to four years transportation by the Sessions Court, and the sentence was upheld by the High Court of Madras on 4 November 1908.[18]

In the meantime, the rival moderate and extremist factions had a very public falling out at the Surat session of the Indian National Congress in 1907. First, the venue of the session was shifted from Nagpur to Surat, to the displeasure of the nationalist faction. Second, the nationalist faction wanted Lala Lajpat Rai to be the president of the session but this wish was thwarted by the moderates who ensured that Rash Bihari Ghosh was appointed as the president instead. Tilak wished to address the session on this issue, which was not allowed, resulting in an outbreak of violence with delegates assaulting each other. In an unfortunate turn of events, a participant hurled a shoe at Phirozeshah Mehta and Surendranath Banerji in the chaos. In the aftermath of the internal conflict, the Indian National Congress split up, with the nationalists led by Tilak parting way with the moderates.[19]

Alarmed by the rise in revolutionary nationalism, the government enacted the Prevention of Seditious Meetings Act on 1 November 1907[20] which sought to prevent public meetings likely to promote sedition or cause disturbance of public tranquillity. The Act mandated that no public meeting for the furtherance or discussion of any subject likely to cause disturbance or political excitement, or of any political subject, or for the exhibition or distribution of any writing or printed matter relating to any such subject shall be held without written notice of such meeting and only after obtaining permission for the same. People were not allowed to hold meetings in areas proclaimed to be out of bounds for such meetings by the government, and no one was allowed to deliver any speech at such prohibited meetings. Any contravention of the Act was punishable by a sentence of six months' imprisonment or a fine, or both. The Act was valid for a term of three years.

Towards the end of 1907, the revolutionaries of Bengal ventured on the path of political assassinations. A train carrying Sir Andrew Fraser, the lieutenant governor of Bengal, was sabotaged and attacked on 7 December 1907 at Naraingarh in Midnapore, Bengal. The attack proved unsuccessful but announced the escalation of revolutionary violence in Bengal. The revolutionaries were trained and indoctrinated at secret societies which took the form of gymnasiums, athletic clubs, social organizations, etc. The prominent leaders of this movement were the brothers Aurobindo Ghosh and Barindra Ghosh, along with Bipin Chandra Pal and Jatindra Nath Banerjee among others.[21]

In early 1908, an attempt on the life of Douglas Kingsford, the chief presidency magistrate of Calcutta, was made. Kingsford was unpopular for the harsh punishments he meted out to Swadeshi activists. On one occasion, he passed a sentence against a young boy of fifteen named Sushil Sen who had been picketing the court during Swadeshi demonstrations. He was punished with fifteen lashes in public view, which he tolerated with cries of 'Bande Mataram'. The incident caused major outrage and was reported in all newspapers across Bengal. In retribution against this act, the revolutionaries devised a 'book bomb' which was sent as a package to the residence of Kingsford in Calcutta. However, under the belief that it was just a book being returned by one of his friends, he did not open the package, thus unwittingly foiling the plan.[22]

In the meantime, the government got a hint of plans to assassinate Kingsford and as a safeguard transferred him to Muzaffarpur which was in north Bihar. Two young revolutionaries named Khudiram Bose and Prafulla Chaki were sent after him in April 1908. There, they planned to assassinate him by bombing his carriage, but mistook a different carriage as Kingsford's. The carriage in fact belonged to a barrister named Pringle Kennedy, and Bose and Chaki blew up a wrong carriage: the one which was actually carrying Mrs Kennedy and their daughter, thereby killing them. Khudiram Bose was hanged for this crime in August 1908, Chaki having committed suicide on being arrested for the murder.[23]

Interestingly, Kingsford had a third lease of life when conspirators of the Muzaffarpur incident revealed the 'book bomb' assassination plot in January 1909. Kingsford was immediately informed about the plot upon which he discovered the bomb which he had carried to Muzaffarpur from Calcutta, the package still unopened![24]

The second trial of Bal Gangadhar Tilak took place in this context.[25]

Tilak was fresh from his break as the leader of the new party opposed to the moderates of the Indian National Congress. *Kesari* enjoyed a great boost to its circulation post his first trial and became one of the most prominent voices of the new party. Tilak was also considered to have become a nationalist leader with a pan-Indian appeal with his call for Swarajya.

On 12 May 1908, *Kesari* published an article titled 'The Country's Misfortune' followed by another article titled 'These Remedies Are Not Lasting' published on 9 June.[26]

The first article was written on the subject of the Muzaffarpur incident. The article described the incident and blamed it on the 'perversity of the white official class', which referred to the British government. It compared the state of affairs to the Russian Revolution of 1905 where the oppressed were exasperated into throwing bombs.

The second article was about the practice of bomb-throwing and it pointed out that it was the most mischievous thing to do, that people in other countries had obtained what they want by hurling bombs.

Bombay Police received sanction from the governor of Bombay to prosecute Tilak for being the editor, publisher and proprietor of *Kesari*. The police filed information of the first article before A.H.S. Aston, the chief presidency magistrate of Bombay, on 24 June. Tilak was arrested that same evening from Sardar Griha near Crawford Market in Bombay after a warrant for his arrest was issued by the magistrate.

Incidentally, Tilak was present in Bombay to help Shivram Paranjpe, the editor of *Kal,* who was being prosecuted for sedition for publishing an article related to the Muzaffarpur bombing incident. The article said:

People are prepared to do anything for the sake of Swarajya and they no longer sing the glories of British rule. They have no dread of British power. It is simply a question of sheer brute force. Bomb-throwing in India is different from bomb-throwing in Russia. Many of the Russians side with their Government against these bomb-throwers, but it is doubtful whether much sympathy will be found in India . . . Setting aside the question whether bomb-throwing is justifiable or not, Indians are not trying to promote disorder but to obtain Swarajya.

Paranjpe was convicted for sedition on 8 July 1908.

Tilak was produced before the magistrate on 25 June, and an unsuccessful plea for his release on bail was moved by Jehangir Dinshaw Davar, barrister, and Mahadeo Bodas, pleader of the high court.

The Bombay Police along with the Poona Police searched the residence and office of Tilak in Poona on 25 June and discovered a card in his office with 'Handbook of modern explosives by M. Eissler published by Crossby Lockwood & Sons' and 'Nitro-explosives by P. Gerad Sanford' printed on one side, and 'Modern Explosives by Esiel Explosives by Crosby and Lockwood' printed on the other side.

On 26 June, the governor sanctioned another prosecution against Tilak with regard to the second article, followed by information being filed before the chief presidency magistrate on 27 June. An arrest warrant was issued again and Tilak was nominally arrested in Dongri jail where he was being lodged since 24 June.

Based on the two articles, the Bombay government launched a prosecution against Tilak for sedition under Section 124A, and promotion of enmity between classes under Section 153A of the IPC. The information under Sections 124A and 153A alleged that Tilak had by publication of the articles 'brought or attempted to bring into hatred and contempt and has excited or attempted to excite disloyalty and feelings of enmity towards His Majesty and the Government established by law in British India and has also attempted to promote feelings of enmity and hatred between the English and Indian subjects of His Majesty'. The magistrate committed the case for trial before the high court on 29 June.

Another bail application was filed before the Bombay High Court on 2 July on behalf of Tilak. The judge hearing this plea was Justice Dinshaw Davar, father of Tilak's lawyer, Jehangir Davar, and himself Tilak's erstwhile lawyer who had represented him in bail proceedings during his first sedition trial in 1897!

Tilak was represented by Muhammad Ali Jinnah[27] in the bail proceedings before Justice Davar. Jinnah argued that Tilak was under trial and his enlargement on bail was necessary to help him conduct his defence properly. Tilak faced hindrance in instructing his counsel while in prison as he believed that the translations of his articles were inaccurate. He was also being treated for diabetes which would make his time in jail difficult. Jinnah pointed out that Tilak was a highly educated individual with great social stature which was underlined by his term as a member of the Legislative Council. Jinnah pointed out the objections to certain affidavits filed on behalf of the prosecution as being prejudicial to Tilak's case. Justice Davar responded by asking Jinnah to argue as if he was arguing ex parte, which means arguing in the absence of the opposite party. In fact, Davar went to the extent of saying, 'I will not trouble you, Mr Advocate General' when James Branson, the acting advocate general, attempted to address the court.

Jinnah persisted in pleading that to ensure the conduct of a fair trial, it was important to release Tilak, as had been done earlier in his first trial by Justice Tyabji. What was left unsaid was that Dinshaw Davar himself had argued the 1897 bail application, so he was expected to have a view consistent with the arguments in that case.

In deciding the application, Justice Davar said that he personally felt unwilling in keeping an under-trial person in prison and recognized that the court had a great amount of discretion in deciding bail applications. However, he felt that the only question in deciding a bail application was not just whether an accused would turn up in court for his trial or not if released on bail. He was of the view that other circumstances must also be considered, but did not state what was on his mind as he purportedly did not want to prejudice the jury even before the trial began. He rejected the bail application without providing reasons, as he was afraid that the matter was the focus of the press at that time, and his reasons might be printed and circulated to the public. Justice Davar thus contradicted himself because he had argued to the contrary when he applied for bail for Tilak in 1897 before Justice Tyabji. Consequently, Tilak was consigned to face trial as a prisoner.

The next day, the prosecution applied for the empanelment of a special jury for Tilak's trial. A special jury meant that most of the jurors would be Europeans as opposed to a common jury comprised mostly of Indians. Tilak's lawyer in this instance was Joseph Baptista, barrister. He raised a spirited objection to the empanelment of a European-majority special jury as it was prejudicial to Tilak's defence. An Indian-majority jury would have been better suited to try Tilak because the articles in *Kesari* were in Marathi, and Tilak felt that the translations were wanting in nuance and accuracy and therefore not reliable. Europeans would have to go by whatever the official translations were while Indian jurors would not have felt the necessity to rely on translations due to their knowledge of Marathi. Further, the political nature of the trial also made a European jury unconducive for the trial.

Justice Davar did not find any merit in the opposition to a special jury and directed that a special jury with at least half the jurors being European be empanelled. He felt it was so required because the case was of great importance and required a jury selected from citizens of Bombay but from a higher class. The racial undertone, especially coming from an Indian judge, was remarkable but unfortunately par for the course at that time. Davar also directed that the official translations be relied upon in ordinary course, but assured Baptista that he would ensure application of mind whenever any glaring error was pointed out by the defence. A special jury comprising of seven Europeans and two Indians was eventually empanelled.

The modalities having been concluded, the trial began on 13 July 1908. The prosecution was represented by James Branson, the acting advocate general, with John Inverarity as barrister. Tilak famously acted in his own defence, having been constrained by his incarceration.

At the outset, Branson proposed to try Tilak for both the articles together, even though the charges were framed by the magistrate separately. He claimed that it would be more convenient to do so rather than have two trials before two separate juries. Towards this end, he decided to prosecute Tilak under Section 153A of the IPC against the second article only, which was 'The Remedies Are Not Lasting', and dropped the charge with regard to the first article. Therefore, Tilak was tried for two charges of sedition under Section 124A and one charge of promoting enmity between classes under Section 153A.

Tilak opposed the proposal for consolidation because the two articles were on separate subjects and therefore required separate trials. He displayed his inability to conduct his defence in two trials together. Justice Davar, however, allowed the consolidation of the trial conditional upon only three charges being prosecuted upon. He also found that the consolidation would be in the interest of the accused despite Tilak's submission to the contrary!

The prosecution began with a reading of the first article, 'The Country's Misfortune', which pertained to the Muzaffarpur incident. It claimed that the article meant to imply that the British rule was governed by self-interest, except insofar as it is restricted by the need to prevent the exasperation of its Indian subjects. The article advocated that the power to govern should be taken out of the hands of the British and put into the hands of Indians. It claimed that the

people wanted *swarajya,* which meant self-government or
self-rule, and advocated the methods used by Russians to be
used by Indians towards attaining swarajya, which included
bombings. The prosecution contended that the writer of
the article claimed to represent 300 million Indians burning
with indignation and suggested that it is possible that
some people can be expected to commit outrages induced
by the oppressive system of government. The prosecution
pointed out that it was defamatory against the government
to suggest that the British government was acting for the
benefit of Britain at the expense of the natives of India. The
article compared the Indians to a cat and the government to
a master who treats it with cruelty. In that scenario, it said,
it was only natural that the cat would pounce on its master
with intent to kill.

Therefore, in summary, the prosecution argued that the
article sought to convey 'that the only thing which comes
between the people of India and the blessings of this country
is the English rule'. In light of the same, the prosecution
contended that Tilak was guilty of sedition under Section
124A of the IPC.

With regard to the second article, the prosecution
contended that it made a veiled suggestion that other
countries 'enjoyed the advantages of use of bombs and
assassination', and that bombs could easily be made
even in India. It again called the British government a
selfish administration as it was devoted to the benefit of
Englishmen and not to the benefit of Indians. It said that
a bomb 'is a charm, an amulet' which protected Indians
from total exploitation by the government for the benefit
of England's enrichment. The British government was a
curse upon the people of India, it argued. The prosecution
argued that Tilak was guilty of sedition under Section
124A of the IPC because of the attack on the government.

Additionally, it was contended that Tilak was also guilty of promoting enmity between Englishmen and Indians which was punishable under Section 153A of the code.

Upon examination of witnesses by the prosecution, and their cross-examination by Tilak, it became clear that the Marathi to English translations relied upon by the prosecution were wildly inaccurate and contrary to the context. Tilak addressed the court on 15 July by pointing out that the Marathi terminology in the discussion of political subjects was not settled at that time, and therefore the translations of the articles were not accurate.

Further, he enunciated his views on the political reforms required in India, calling for greater inclusion of Indians in the administration of the country, without which estrangement of the native population was inevitable. He said:

> The mere shifting of the centre of power and authority from one official to another is not, in my opinion, calculated to restore the feelings of cordiality between officers and people prevailing in earlier days. English education has created new aspirations and ideals amongst the people and so long as these national aspirations remain unsatisfied it is useless to expect that the hiatus between the officers and the people could be removed by any scheme of official Decentralization, whatever its other effects may be. It is no remedy—not even palliative—against the evil complained of, nor was it put forward by the people or their leaders. The fluctuating wave of Decentralization may infuse more or less life in the individual members of the Bureaucracy, but it cannot remove the growing estrangement

between the rulers and the ruled, unless and until
the people are allowed more and more effective
voice in the management of their own affairs in
an ever expansive spirit of wise liberalism and
wide sympathy aiming at raising India to the level
of the self-governing country.

Tilak demanded that the prosecution be asked to point out
the exact passages from the articles for which he was being
prosecuted but was told by the court that the prosecution
will not be compelled to specify the passages. In fact, the
court went one step ahead and made entire articles a part of
the charges against Tilak.

Tilak told the court that in such circumstances he would
be constrained to give a very long address to the jury in his
defence. The court permitted him to do so, which was ironic
as the court earlier did not compel the advocate general to
point out specific passages in the articles because he did not
want to tire out the jury!

The court clearly had no inkling of what was in store
for them.

Tilak's speech, one of the most celebrated in Indian
political history, commenced on 15 July (Wednesday),
which was the third day of the trial, and concluded only on
the eighth day of the trial, which was 22 July. The duration
of the speech was about twenty-one hours, according to
notes kept by Justice Davar. A break over the weekend was
the only breather for the jury when they were excused to
tend to their mail!

He read out Section 124A of the IPC for the benefit of
the jury and said:

This section is divided into two parts. The first part
refers to actually bringing into hatred or contempt

His Majesty, etc. But as there is no evidence before the Court that any excitement has been caused by the articles in question, so it seems to me that the prosecution does not mean to proceed under that part of the section. The second part of the section deals with 'attempts to excite disaffection'. The section does not simply refer to the publication of anything likely to create disaffection . . . Attempt is actually an offence, minus the final act of crime. The mere fact that a certain article is published will not make it an attempt. There must be a criminal mind, a culpable indifference to consequences. In the present case, there has been no evidence to prove that the attempt failed because the Government interfered or because the people refused to listen. Attempt includes both motives and intention . . . Criminal intention cannot be presumed but must be positively proved by the evidence of surrounding circumstances . . . If the writer's motives are good, if he is trying to secure constitutional rights for the people, trying in a fair way and persevering manner, he is entitled to express his views fully and fearlessly . . . the mere fact that the views of the writer are not correct, or are even absurd, or that he expressed them in violent language, would not make him seditious.[28]

Tilak contended that his articles were in response to the Anglo-Indian press and pro-government parties who tried to lay the blame for the Muzaffarpur bomb outrage at the feet of the Congress. His articles were suggestions to the government and addressed to it to discuss the situation and criticize measures taken by the government. He claimed to not have said anything that others in the press had not already said. Tilak's prosecution was just limited to a charge of exciting disaffection amongst the Marathi-speaking population, but he contended that other Marathi newspapers had also said the same thing. Therefore, he questioned the government's motives in prosecuting him and argued that such prosecution was unjustifiable.

He beseeched the jury by invoking future generations which would look to their verdict to determine whether Tilak was judged rightly or not. He assured the jury that even if one of them came forward with a not-guilty verdict he would feel satisfied. He asked them to rise to the cause which he represented and arrive at the right decision.

Branson followed Tilak with a four-hour-long address to the jury and liberally indulged in ad hominem against him. He rubbished Tilak's defence and demanded that he be convicted for the offences he was charged for. Justice Davar followed it with a hurried charge to the jury which was adverse to Tilak's defence. Unsurprisingly, the jury returned a finding of guilt with a 7–2 majority and convicted Tilak for sedition for causing enmity between Englishmen and Indians.

Justice Davar afforded an opportunity to Tilak to make a statement before his sentence was pronounced. Tilak famously said:

> All I wish to say is that in spite of the verdict of the jury, I maintain that I am innocent. There are higher powers that rule the destinies of things; and it may well be the will of the providence that the cause which I represent may prosper more by my sufferings than by my remaining free.[29]

The dignity of the statement was met with an extremely harsh response from Justice Davar who said:

It seems to me that it must be a diseased mind, a most perverted intellect that could say that the articles which you have written are legitimate weapons in political agitation. They are seething with sedition, they preach violence; they speak of murders with approval; and the cowardly and atrocious act of committing murders with bombs not only seems to meet with your approval, but you hail the advent of the bomb in India as if something has come to India for its good . . . Your hatred of the ruling class has not disappeared during these ten years.[30] And in these articles . . . you wrote about bombs as if they were legitimate instruments in political agitation. Such journalism is a curse to the country. I feel much sorrow in sentencing you . . . Having regard to your age and circumstances, I think it is most desirable, in the interest of peace and order and in the interest of the country which you profess to love, that you should be out of it for some time.[31]

Thus, on 22 July 1908, Tilak was sentenced to three years' transportation each for two counts of sedition under Section 124A of the IPC, which would run consecutively, thereby totalling six years' transportation. He was also fined Rs 1000 for the third charge under Section 153A of the code. Tilak turned fifty-three the next day.

He was first taken to Sabarmati jail in Gujarat on 23 July and eventually transported to Mandalay in Burma on 13 September 1908 to serve out his sentence in a 240 square feet cell. In the meantime, Tilak lost his appeals before the full bench of the Bombay High Court and subsequently before the Privy Council in England.[32]

Another trial of note which took place in 1909—the outcome of which had far-reaching consequences—was the

case of *Emperor v. Ganesh Damodar Savarkar*.[33] Ganesh
Savarkar, better known as Babarao Savarkar, was the elder
brother of the more illustrious Vinayak Savarkar, also
known as Veer Savarkar. Ganesh Savarkar, along with
Vinayak, was a founding member of Abhinav Bharat ('new
India'), a group of young revolutionaries formed in Nashik
in present-day Maharashtra. Savarkar was a close associate
of Tilak and had been arrested when he went to Bombay
to help Paranjpe with the *Kal* sedition trial. This was about
the same time in June 1908 when Tilak was arrested for
sedition when he was also in Bombay to help Paranjpe. He
served a month's imprisonment in the same jail as Tilak.[34]

Savarkar was again arrested while he was in Bombay
on 28 February 1909 and taken to Nashik to stand trial
for abetting the waging of war against the emperor (Section
121 of the IPC) and for sedition. The offences arose from
the publication of four poems out of eighteen in *Laghu
Abhinava Bharat Mala*, which translates to 'A short series
for new India'. They were written by the poet Govind
and were based on mythology and history. However, the
court was of the view that the poems actually encouraged
Indians to get rid of British rule by taking up arms against
the government. There were allusions in the poems referring
to 'black' people being ruled by 'white' people, and talked
about the destruction of foreign demons by Krishna and
Shivaji.

Another poem invoked the deity Ganesha and asked him
to take up his sword against 'demons of subjection' which
had spread lamentation all across the world. On 8 June
1909, Justice B.C. Kennedy, the sessions judge of Nashik,
convicted Savarkar for sedition and abetment of waging of
war against the emperor (Section 121) on the basis of the
said poems. Savarkar was sentenced to transportation for
life for the offence under Section 121 of the code and for

two years' imprisonment for the offence of sedition to run simultaneously with the first sentence.

An appeal was filed before the Bombay High Court where Ganesh Savarkar was represented by Joseph Baptista, Tilak's associate and lawyer. The High Court, while confirming his conviction on 8 November 1909, said:

> No doubt the writer has used several words, each having a double meaning, but that meaning only serves to emphasise the fact that the writer's main object is to preach war against the recent Government, in the names of certain Gods of the Hindus and certain warriors such as Shivaji. Those names are mere pretexts for the text which is: Take up the sword and destroy the Government because it is foreign and oppressive. For the purpose of finding the motive and intention of the writer it is unnecessary to import into the interpretation of the poems sentiments or ideas borrowed from the Bhagwad Gita. The poems afford their own interpretation, and no one who knows Marathi can or will understand them as preaching anything but war against the British Government. Mr Baptista has conceded that of the poems be construed as referring to the British Government, they fall within the meaning of sedition under section 124A of the Indian Penal Code. That they are such as to excite disaffection goes without saying . . . Briefly summarised, the teaching of this book is that India must have independence: that otherwise, she will be unworthy of herself: that independence cannot be obtained without armed rebellion and that, therefore, the Indians ought to take arms and rebel. This is quite plain

though the teaching is thinly veiled by allusions to mythology and history. It is sedition of a gross kind and very little attempt was made to show that the conviction under section 124A of the Indian Penal Code was not correct.[35]

Ganesh Savarkar was convicted to transportation for life and subsequently incarcerated in the dreaded Cellular Jail in the Andamans. The response to his conviction was immediate and violent. On 1 July 1909, Madan Lal Dhingra, an Indian revolutionary, shot and killed Colonel William Curzon Wyllie in England. A statement discovered on him when he was arrested read: 'I attempted to shed English blood intentionally and of purpose as an humble protest against the inhuman transportations and hangings of Indian youths.'[36] This was followed by the murder of Jackson, the district magistrate of Nashik, on 21 December 1909 because he was the one who had committed Ganesh Savarkar to the Sessions Court for trial.[37]

As the Prevention of Seditious Meeting Act, 1907, finished its three-year term in 1910, another identical and namesake Act was brought about in 1911 to revive the deceased 1907 Act. The Prevention of Seditious Meeting Act, 1911 lived up to the grand old age of 107 years, with post-Independence amendments, and was finally put to rest by the Repealing and Amending (Second) Act, 2017 with effect from 4 January 2018. Ravi Shankar Prasad, the law minister of India, while replying to a debate on the passage of the repealing Act, said that old and irrelevant pre-Independence colonial laws were an unfortunate part of our colonial legacy and repealing them was a progressive move that reflected the 'pro-reform' approach of his government.[38] The irony of this statement will be clearer in a later chapter.

As Hirendranath Mukherjee notes in *India's Struggle for Freedom*,[39] Vladimir Lenin summed up the first decade of twentieth-century India saying:

> In India the native slaves of the 'civilised' British capitalists have recently been causing their 'masters' a lot of unpleasantness and disquietude . . . the Indian masses are beginning to come out into the streets in defence of their native writers and political leaders. The despicable sentence that the English jackals passed on the Indian democrat Tilak . . . this act of vengeance against a democrat on the part of the lackeys of the moneybags, gave rise to street demonstrations and a strike in Bombay. And the Indian proletariat too has already matured sufficiently to wage a class-conscious and political mass struggle . . . The class conscious workers of Europe now have Asiatic comrades and their number will grow by leaps and bounds.

In introducing the Press Act of 1910, Sir Herbert Risley, a member of the Legislative Council, said:

> Sedition has the monopoly of its audience, and that audience is large, and is increasing daily . . . The consequences of this ever-flowing stream of slander and incitement to outrage are now upon us. What was dimly foreseen a few years ago has actually come to pass. We are at the present moment confronted with a murderous conspiracy, whose aim is to subvert the Government of the country, and to make British rule impossible by establishing general terrorism. Their organization is effective and far-reaching; their numbers are believed to be

considerable; the leaders work in secret and are blindly obeyed by their youthful followers . . . There is plenty of work in India waiting to be done, but it never will be done if the energies of the educated classes are wasted in incessant abuse and suspicion of Government.[40]

6

Dark Acts and the Black Act

Things became so bad (for the British) that on 10 December 1917 Lord Chelmsford, the governor general of India, decided to appoint a committee to investigate and report on the nature and extent of 'criminal conspiracies' connected with the revolutionary movement in India, and to examine and consider the difficulties which arose for the British government as a result of the revolutionary movement. The committee was tasked with advising the government on the enactment of legislation to tackle the problem. Justice Sidney Rowlatt[1] was given the presidentship of the committee, as a 'strong judicial element' was considered necessary for proper examination of the questions raised by the government. The other members of the committee were Sir Basil Scott,[2] Diwan Bahadur C.V.K. Sastri,[3] Sir Verney Lovett[4] and Provash Chandra Mitter.[5] The committee was directed to assemble in Calcutta in January 1918 to commence work and was given access to all documentary evidence in possession of the government pertaining to the existence and extent of the revolutionary movement in India.[6]

The committee duly assembled in January 1918 and carried out its mandate over a period of four months. It held forty-six sittings, out of which forty-two were held in Calcutta and four in Lahore. The sittings were in camera away from the public gaze and in secret. The governments of Bengal, Bombay, Madras, Bihar and Orissa, Central Provinces, United Provinces, Punjab and Burma along with the government of India placed documentary evidence before the committee. In many cases, documentary evidence was supported by personal testimonies from government officials and, in some cases, members of the public who did not hold any official position. The report of the Sedition Committee was presented to the secretary of the Home Department of the government of India on 15 April 1918 by Justice Rowlatt.[7]

In the summary of conclusions at Chapter XV of the report, the Sedition Committee stated that after investigating all the conspiracies connected with the revolutionary movement, it reached the conclusion that the Bombay revolutionaries were purely Brahmin and mostly Chitpavan Brahmin. The Bengal revolutionaries were mostly educated young men from the middle class whose propaganda had been elaborate, persistent and ingenious, resulting in murders and robberies. According to the report, in Punjab most revolutionaries were returning emigrants from America who indulged in bloodshed and caused the Ghadar Movement of 1915. The committee found that the revolutionary movement largely failed to take root in the Central Provinces, United Provinces, Madras, Bihar and Orissa. However, Burma was somewhat affected by the Ghadar Movement, but it was contained by the government. It will be worthwhile to take a brief look at the findings of the Sedition Committee with regard to revolutionary activities in Bombay, Bengal, Punjab and Madras since the turn of the twentieth century.

The report noted that the first conviction of Tilak in 1897 for sedition did not put an end to seditious writings by the vernacular press in Bombay. In fact, Shivraj Mahadeo Paranjpe, an associate of Tilak, started publishing a vernacular titled *Kal.* The seditious contents of *Kal* led to Paranjpe's arrest in 1899 but he was released with a warning. He again risked prosecution for sedition in 1900, 1904, 1905 and 1907 but the government for some reason left him alone despite seriously considering action against him. He was finally tried and convicted for sedition in 1908. Another vernacular newspaper which faced prosecutions for sedition was *Vihari.* Three successive editors of *Vihari* were tried and convicted for sedition in 1906, 1907 and 1908.[8]

At the same time, London also became a centre of revolutionary movement with the foundation of the India Home Rule Society by Shyamaji Krishnavarma in 1905. Krishnavarma had gone from Bombay to London to set up the society with the object of securing Home Rule for India and for it to serve as a machine to spread awareness about the Indian cause in England. Amongst one of the early members of the society was Vinayak Damodar Savarkar, better known as Veer Savarkar. He was the younger brother of Ganesh Savarkar, whose trial for sedition has been discussed in the previous chapter. He joined the society in 1906. The base of operations of the society set up by Krishnavarma in London was called India House. According to the Sedition Committee report, India House became a 'centre of sedition', drawing attention to the society. A question was raised in the British House of Commons in July 1907 inquiring what the government planned to do about Krishnavarma. Due to the heat on him, Krishnavarma relocated to Paris. By 1909, Vinayak Savarkar rose to the leadership of India House. The 'Indian Sociologist', the mouthpiece of the society, was prosecuted for sedition in England and its editors imprisoned in July and September 1909. All this was about the same time as Ganesh Savarkar's

conviction for sedition in 1909 after which Madan Lal
Dhingra assassinated Sir William Curzon Willie in London
as retribution. Dhingra was also a member of India
House.[9]

Vinayak Savarkar, enraged by his brother's
incarceration, escalated anti-British activities and entrusted
copies of a pamphlet titled 'Vande Mataram' to an associate
to be distributed in Bombay. The pamphlet was in support
of Madan Lal Dhingra and called upon Indians to 'Terrorise
the officials, English and Indian, and the collapse of the
whole machinery of oppression is not very far'. It advocated
separate political assassinations as the 'best conceivable
method of paralysing the bureaucracy and arousing the
masses'. However, the carrier of the pamphlets was arrested
upon his arrival in Bombay.[10]

The report also noted the activities and prosecution
of secret societies like Abhinav Bharat in Nashik and
Satara and Nav Bharat in Gwalior. It concluded that the
first revolutionary crime was the Rand murder in Pune
in 1897, subsequent to which Tilak was prosecuted for
sedition for the first time, and that revolutionary crimes
had grown due to revolutionary activities of Brahmins
of the region. It attributed most activities to Chitpavan
Brahmins, who, the report claimed, were ultra-orthodox
and consequently anti-Muslim and anti-British. The
committee squarely laid the blame on the Poona vernacular
press for its anti-British writings and recognized Tilak as
the leader of the 'Poona extremists'.[11]

About Bengal, the report discussed the history of the
revolutionary movement in the region and the partition of
Bengal. Both these aspects have already been written about
in the previous chapter. However, mention must be made
of the secret societies of East Bengal which were declared
unlawful in January 1909. These societies were the Dacca

Anusilan Samiti, Swadesh Bandhab Samiti, Brati Samiti, Suhrid Samiti and Sadhana Samiti. They took the form of youth associations but secretly carried out revolutionary and seditious activities and inflicted major damage upon the British government. The revolutionary movement in Bengal finally drove the government to reunify East and West Bengal into a single entity by the end of 1911. Nevertheless, revolutionary activities in reunified Bengal continued beyond 1911.[12]

In one instance, on 26 June 1916, a group of revolutionaries calling themselves the Western Bengal Party robbed a house in Calcutta and allegedly stole Rs 11,500. Two days later, the victim received a letter titled 'Bande Mataram' from the 'Bengal Branch of Independent Kingdom of United India' saying, 'Gentlemen, Six honorary officers of our Calcutta Finance Department have taken a loan of Rs 9,891.1.5 from you, and have deposited the amount in the office noted above on your account to fulfil our great aim. The sum has been entered in our ca book on your name at 5 per cent per annum. By the grace of God if we be successful we will pay the whole amount with the interest at one time.' The letter, signed by one J. Balamanta, the 'Finance Secretary to the Bengal Branch of Independent Kingdom of United India', also vowed to return two valuable items which they realized were pledged to someone by the victim within two weeks![13]

It is unclear whether they followed up on their promise or not as they were arrested within a month of the robbery.

The First World War (1914–18) and the years leading up to it brought Indian revolutionaries close to the Germans who shared their anti-British sentiments. The committee noted that Friedrich von Bernhardi[14] in his 1911 book, *Germany and the Next War*, had hoped for the Hindu and Mohammedan nationalists of Bengal (and India) to combine forces to 'create a very grave danger capable of shaking the foundations of England's high position in the world'.[15]

In fact, in October 1914, one Chempakaraman Pillai started working with the German Foreign Office in Berlin and set up the 'Indian National Party', which included Lala Hardayal, Taraknath Das, Barkatulla, Chandra K. Chakrabarti and Heramba Lal Gupta. Their main task was to create and disseminate anti-British propaganda and to turn Indian prisoners of war captured from the British army towards the German cause. From 1914 onwards, there was a concerted effort by the Germans to help organize an uprising in Bengal by helping Indian revolutionaries with the supply of weapons and cash via sea and land. The plot was foiled by the British government, and finally all attempts to procure arms from the Germans were abandoned by the Bengal revolutionaries.[16]

In Punjab, the committee reported that by 1907 there were attempts in Amritsar and Ferozepur to arouse feelings of disloyalty, which were considerably successful. Seditious meetings and propaganda were widespread in Rawalpindi, Sialkot, Lyallpur and Lahore, the hub of the anti-British campaign in Punjab. In introducing the Prevention of Seditious Meeting Bill, 1907, the Indian viceroy told the Legislative Council:

> We cannot afford to forget the events of the early spring, the riots at Lahore and gratuitous insults to Europeans, the Pindi riots, the serious view of the Lieutenant-Governor of Punjab on the state of his province, the consequent arrest of Lajpat Rai and Ajit Singh, and the promulgation of the Ordinance, and contemporaneously will all this, a daily story from Eastern Bengal of assault, of looting, of boycotting and general lawlessness, encouraged by agitators,

who with an utter disregard for consequences,
no matter how terrible, have by public addresses,
by seditious newspapers, by seditious leaflets,
by itinerant secret agents, lost no opportunity of
inflaming the worst passions of racial feelings.[17]

Revolutionaries from Punjab found their way to America
in 1911. Lala Hardayal, an associate of Krishnavarma and
Vinayak Savarkar, set up a press in San Francisco called
Jugantar Asram, which published the anti-British newspaper
called *Ghadr,* which means 'mutiny'. The multilingual
newspaper was widely circulated amongst Indians in
America and forwarded to India, where it preached
mutiny against the British. His organization was called
the Ghadr Party, which found wings both in America and
Canada, with the large Sikh immigrant population in the
latter country adding to the numbers. Many of the Ghadr
revolutionaries started returning to India on Japanese ships
during the First World War but were impeded by the British
government which had received intelligence on the party.
The government promulgated an ordinance restricting the
entry of the emigrants to arrest them upon arrival, or if
they acted suspiciously. The Ingress into India Ordinance
took away the right to trial and right to appeal in order
to expedite the prosecution of revolutionaries and 'sedition-
mongers'. It attempted to ensure prompt suppression of
revolutionary activities.[18]

However, the government needed stronger measures
in order to counter revolutionary and seditious activities
in Bengal and Punjab, for which it enacted the Defence of
India Act, 1915, which was swiftly passed by the Legislative
Council. The Act reiterated the provisions of the ordinance
and took away the right to trial and appeal from persons
accused of seditious activities. It established Special Tribunals

for the trial of revolutionary crimes. Known as the Lahore Conspiracy Trials, nine batches of revolutionaries were tried by the Special Tribunals established by the Defence of India Act, resulting in twenty-eight hangings and numerous transportations and imprisonments.[19]

On seditious literature, the judgment in the first case stated, 'There is no doubt the establishment of a press in India was one of the methods they intended to further their designs. The success in seducing people which the Ghadr had attained in America was sufficient encouragement for this course to be adopted in India; and it is common knowledge that Indians are easily swayed by that which is print.' The judgment in the second case found that sedition was actively preached in the villages of Punjab and among regiments of Indian soldiers. It stated, '*Ghadr* newspaper and its progeny (verses, leaflets, etc.) were distributed in every place where the revolutionaries hoped to gain adherents, and particularly among troops.' The Sedition Committee found that the Ghadr Movement could not have been suppressed quickly without the Defence of India Act and the Ingress Ordinance as any delay in preventive actions and punishments would have increased the problems of the British government.[20]

Special mention must be made of seditious activities in Madras, parts of which have been discussed in the previous chapter. The committee noted the seditious activities of a Tamil newspaper named *India* which was published in Madras. Its editor, Srinivas Iyengar, was convicted for sedition by the Madras High Court for publishing three articles in May and June 1908. This forced the newspaper to shut shop in Madras. The publication of the newspaper was moved to Pondicherry from where it continued seditious publications with added vigour. At about the same time, one Nilakanta Brahmachari travelled across southern India along with Shankar Krishna Aiyar propagating the ideas of

Swadeshi and preaching sedition. Their ranks were joined by V.V.S. Aiyar, a close associate of Vinayak Savarkar at India House, who travelled to Pondicherry via Paris and taught revolver shooting to revolutionaries. A press called the Feringhi Destroyer Press published seditious pamphlets and called for the banishment of foreigners from India and the establishment of Swarajya. Things came to a head in June 1911 when one Vanchi Aiyer, an official of the Travancore kingdom, assassinated the district magistrate of Tinnevelly[21] in a railway carriage. He was aided by Shankar Krishna Aiyar who was also arrested for the assassination. He carried with him a letter stating that every Indian was trying to drive out the English to restore Swarajya and Sanatana Dharma.[22]

In July 2011, Madame Bhikaji Cama, a leading Indian revolutionary based in Paris, wrote in her publication called *Bande Mataram*, 'When the gilded slaves from Hindustan were parading the streets of London as performers in the royal circus and were prostrating themselves like so many cows at the feet of the King of England, two young and brave countrymen of ours proved by their daring deeds at Tinnevelly and at Mymensingh that Hindustan is not sleeping.'[23]

The Sedition Committee report blamed the rise of revolutionary activities in southern India on the influence of revolutionaries from Bengal, Paris and Pondicherry, and did not consider the movement in Madras as indigenous. It was of the view that the movement was due to the influence of the Bengal revolutionaries.

The committee also made a note of our old friends, the Wahhabis. As you may recall, the Wahhabi Movement was the most proximate cause for the enactment of Section 124A. It had died down in the second half of the nineteenth century but raised its head again in the second decade of the twentieth. The Wahhabis were also known as the Mujahidin. In February 1915, fifteen students from Lahore dropped out of their colleges and joined the Mujahidin in Kabul. In January 1917, another eight joined the Mujahidin all the way from eastern Bengal. There were other arrests in the North-West Frontier Province, where people were carrying large sums of money they had collected in their native districts for the Mujahidin cause. The cause stemmed from international events. The British did not support Turkey in the Balkan wars in 1912 and 1913, which led to the loss of territories for the Islamic Ottoman Empire due to losses inflicted by the Christian Balkan armies. In 1914, Turkey joined the alliance against Britain which further strengthened Muhammadan resentment against the British government in India.[24]

In August 1916, the British government discovered a conspiracy known as the Silk Letters Conspiracy. It was a plot to disrupt British rule by attacking the north-west frontier, hand in hand with a Muhammadan uprising in the country. The plotters were working in cohorts with members of the Ghadr Party. The conspiracy was named for some letters written on yellow silk intended for people abroad and containing an intention to ally with Turkish forces. The letters fell into the hands of the British and the plot was foiled. The committee reported that this plot established the anxiety of some Muslim revolutionaries in India to provoke sedition and rebellion in the country. The committee stated, 'Always they preach sedition.' However, it also noted that the general Muslim citizenry and a strong government worked as safeguards against the extremists.[25]

The Sedition Committee had two major laments. One, the criminal procedural law led to protracted trials which took months at a time and thus caused delay in convictions.

Two, the trials and convictions for revolutionary crimes did not have a deterring effect on other revolutionaries.

For example, *Jugantar* suffered five prosecutions for sedition between June 1907 and June 1908. However, the imprisonment of its editors and publishers had no lasting effect as they were simply replaced by other individuals. In fact, the sales of *Jugantar* kept increasing to the extent that crowds of people caused obstructions on the streets of Calcutta in their rush to obtain its copies. The Newspapers (Incitement to Offence) Act, 1908, was introduced by the viceroy, who said, 'The seeds of its wickedness have been sown amongst a strangely impressionable and imitative people—seeds that have been daily nurtured by a system of seditious writing and seditious speaking of unparalleled violence, vociferating to beguiled youth that outrage is the evidence of patriotism and its reward a martyr's crown.'[26]

However, as the 1908 Act proved insufficient, the more comprehensive Indian Press Act was enacted in 1910. In moving the 1910 Act, a member of the Legislative Council said, 'These things are the natural and ordinary consequences of the teachings of certain journals. They have prepared the soil on which anarchy flourishes; they have sown the seed, and they are answerable for the crop. This is no mere general statement; the chain of causation is clear. Not only does the campaign of violence date from the change in the tone of the Press, but specific outbursts of incitement have been followed by specific outrages.'[27]

The Sedition Committee laid a large part of the blame for the rise in seditious and revolutionary activities on the 'pernicious operations of the revolutionary press'.[28]

The preventive measures undertaken by the government during the period under review of the committee were deemed to be inadequate. The committee was wary of the fact that preventive enactments were due to be terminated by efflux of time, including the Defence of India Act which was an emergency wartime enactment. With the end of the First World War, the British army units comprising of Indian soldiers, mostly from Punjab, were to be disbanded. The committee feared that it was possible to incite and stir up discontent amongst these returning soldiers.[29]

To that effect, the committee suggested major legislative measures to deal with sedition and revolutionary crimes. It recommended that measures to secure the punishment of seditious crimes may either be brought about by changes in the general law of evidence and procedure applicable to all offences, or by changes in the substantive law of sedition and changes in law of evidence and procedure to specifically deal with such offences.

With regard to changes in the general law of evidence and procedure, the committee was of the view that criminal courts were quite liberal in granting time for the trial and cross-examination of witnesses. The courts rarely interfered in witness deposition so the examination and cross-examination of witnesses took a considerable amount of time. The committee was of the view that this could be curtailed by the courts by preventing irrelevant questions during trial. Another change suggested was the amendment of the Criminal Procedure Code to permit inducement to extract evidence from witnesses by promising protection against harm caused by the criminal acts of others.[30]

After proposing general changes, the committee moved on to making recommendations for changes in criminal procedure to take care of emergent situations. The changes it suggested were specifically for future emergencies and to be deployed at short notice. These emergency measures were supposed to lie in limbo on statute books only to be pressed into action on declaration of emergency by the governor general. While the committee desisted from drafting the form of any such notifications, it felt that it would be sufficient to declare that seditious offences were prevalent due to which it would be expedient to provide for speedy trials to prevent endangering public safety. The committee, however, was awake to the fact that the government should not have the authority to assume powers to take stringent emergency measures without the 'declaration of a crisis of proportionate gravity'.[31]

The committee suggested that crimes of sedition should be tried by a bench of at least three judges, without juries. It also recommended doing away with committal proceedings. Under criminal law, committal is usually the mechanism where a magistrate takes cognizance of a crime and directs the trial of an accused by the appropriate criminal court. The committee felt this was a waste of time and persons accused of seditious offences should be brought directly to trial. Another draconian measure suggested was that the accused should not have the right to appeal against any order of conviction! The flawed logic behind this was that this would have a demoralizing effect and prevent excitement of the disgruntled masses. The Special Tribunals envisaged to carry out trials for sedition were supposed to have judges selected by the chief justice or the head of the court having territorial jurisdiction. It also recommended that the Special Tribunals should be empowered to hold closed-door trials if deemed necessary.[32]

Apart from procedural changes, the committee recommended certain preventive measures to be imposed upon persons who were likely to commit seditious offences. It felt that the government should have power to demand securities, restrict residences, require notification of change of residence, require abstention from acts such as journalism or attending meetings, and require periodic reporting to the police. In addition to this, the committee thought it fit to empower the police to take persons of interest under preventive detention.[33]

In the course of preparing the report, the committee claimed to have gained insight into the minds of revolutionaries and on the movement. The report says:

> These revolutionaries vary widely in character. Some merely require to be kept from evil associations and to be brought under the closer influences of sensible friends or relations. At the other extreme are some desperados at present irreconcilable to the point of frenzy. Some are ready to quit the movement if only it can be made easy for them. More may be brought to this frame of mind in time.[34]

This passage is quite illuminating. The British saw oppressed masses fighting to take back their country as 'evil desperados'!

As a parting shot, clearly a fallout of the Ghadr Movement, the committee suggested the restriction of ingress into India. It was recommended that the government may prohibit or restrict the ingress of Indians returning to their homeland if it deemed it fit to do so to protect the country's safety, interests and tranquillity. It recognized the threat from foreign entities and persons who were purportedly conspiring to cause seditious violence within India.

As mentioned, the Defence of India Act formed the core basis for the Sedition Committee report. The said Act along with other emergency laws had a major impact in Punjab. At the Amritsar session of the Indian National Congress in 1919, Motilal Nehru in his presidential address said, 'The years 1915 to 1917 were occupied with various conspiracy trials by special tribunals constituted under the Defence of India Act. The vernacular press was ruthlessly suppressed and hundreds of persons were interned under the Defence of India Act or the Ingress Ordinance. It was during this period that Lokmanya Tilak and Srijut Bipin Chandra Pal were prohibited from entering the province lest they should introduce the virus of Home Rule here.'[35]

The report amply demonstrates that the age of moderation was past, and nationalists were gaining more ground than the moderates. The extremists who had split from the Congress received a boost with the release of Tilak from prison in 1914, rejoining the Indian National Congress at the session in 1916.

The same year also saw the birth of the Home Rule League in India founded by Annie Besant, a British lady who was the president of the Theosophical Society and a champion of the Indian freedom cause. Another Home Rule League had been established by Tilak to champion the cause of self-government within the British Empire by constitutional means. Tilak undertook a campaign calling for Swaraj by publishing article after article espousing the cause of self-government in his two vernaculars, *Mahratta* and *Kesari*. Tilak's speeches and appeals to the masses earned him the sobriquet 'Lokmanya', which means revered by the masses. Tilak and Besant worked together with Tilak's Home Rule League in Bombay and the Central Provinces and Besant's Home Rule League working in the rest of India.

This invited the third prosecution for sedition against Lokmanya Tilak. He was accused of spreading sedition through his speeches delivered in Marathi while on his lecture tour to spread the message of Home Rule and Swarajya. He was prosecuted for three specific speeches, one at Belgaum on 1 May 1916 and two at Ahmednagar on 31 May and 1 June 1916. However, he was not prosecuted under Section

124A of the IPC as in the earlier two prosecutions.[36] This time he was prosecuted under Section 108 of the Criminal Procedure Code as enacted in 1898, which was the precursor to the current Indian Criminal Procedure Code. Section 108 empowered the chief magistrate in a district or presidency town to call for a surety or bond for good behaviour for a period of at least one year upon receiving information about any persons who, either orally or in writing, disseminate or attempt to disseminate any seditious material which would otherwise be punishable under Section 124A of the IPC.

A large number of lawyers turned up in Tilak's defence before the district magistrate of Poona, with the leader of the defence team being Muhammad Ali Jinnah. The main defence was that Tilak had not attacked the government but had only criticized the bureaucracy, as permitted under Section 124A. The prosecutor, on the other hand, tried to drive home the point that Tilak had been twice convicted of sedition, despite which he was delivering seditious speeches. He also tried to prejudice the judge by telling him that Tilak had attacked the service to which the judge belonged. Tilak told the judge that his lectures intended to explain what the Home Rule Movement was about and were delivered in response to criticism of the movement from various quarters. Jinnah contended that such speeches were protected by Section 124A itself as they sought to bring about change by lawful and constitutional means and did not excite hatred, contempt or disaffection.[37]

However, the court was not impressed with the defence. It directed Tilak to furnish a bond of Rs 20,000 and two sureties of Rs 10,000 each under Section 108 of the Criminal Procedure Code. This direction sought to ensure Tilak's good behaviour for a period of one year. Tilak challenged this order before the Bombay High Court and a bench of Justice Stanley Batchelor and Justice Lallubhai

Shah, both of whom were fluent in Marathi. Here, he was again represented by Jinnah, along with his old friend and lawyer Joseph Baptista. This proved to be a case of 'third time lucky' for Tilak because the High Court sided with him, for a change. It held that upon a careful reading of Tilak's speeches, barring a few isolated passages, it was clear that Tilak was calling for political changes to be obtained by lawful and constitutional means. It concluded that the general effect of the speeches was not seditious and thus set aside the order of the district magistrate.[38]

Annie Besant was not as lucky. The chief presidency magistrate of Madras passed an order on 22 May 1916 declaring the security deposited by *New India*, a publication operated by Annie Besant, to be forfeited under the Indian Press Act, 1910, for publication of seditious articles. Ironically, one of the charges on the publication was that it attacked the Indian Press Act and called it an insult to India and a disgrace to England. It said, 'It is inconsistent with nature and reason. To say it in A.B. Mazumdar's words, it has transformed the editor to a humble suppliant before the District Officer. It should be expunged from the statute book. It is not a law but an oppression.' These statements were in reaction to heavy security being imposed on *New India* under the Press Act due to the activities of Annie Besant in propagating the Home Rule Movement. The articles also attacked the policy of reserving seats and compartments for Europeans on Indian railways. The publication strongly condemned the Anglo-Indian press for being the stooge of the government and for its lack of sympathy for the Indian cause. *New India* was also proving to be a great proponent of the Home Rule Movement and preached methods to achieve it.

All in all, the publication was proving to be a giant thorn in the side for the British government. A number of articles were alleged to be in contravention of Section 4(1) of the Press Act, 1910. The government was of the view that the articles incited murder, violence or other offences under the Explosive Substances Act, 1908; incited sedition by words, signs or visible representations; and incited and encouraged interference with administration of law and maintenance of law and order. The action was challenged by Annie Besant before a special bench of the Madras High Court presided over by Justice Abdur Rahim, Justice William Ayling and Justice Seshagiri Aiyar.[39]

Besant contended that the government did not have the power to deprive her of her property as doing so would be in contravention of the unwritten laws of Great Britain which otherwise protected her by virtue of her being a British subject. She argued that only a court of law could take such an action. She further argued that advocacy for Home Rule does not amount to sedition under Section 124A of the IPC as it is being demanded by lawful means and thus protected under Explanation 2 contained in Section 124A. She further contended that the language of Section 4 of the Press Act was taken from Section 124A and Section 153A of the IPC under which intention to commit an offence is material and must be proved. However, the government contended that intention is immaterial under the Press Act and all that must be seen is whether the general effect of the articles would give rise to a contravention under Section 4 of the Press Act. The government further contended that the High Court did not have the power to interfere with actions taken under the Press Act by virtue of specific provisions in the Act barring such interference.

The court held that it was unnecessary to determine whether the action of the government was illegal or not as the High Court did not have jurisdiction to do so under the Press Act. Therefore, it held that Besant did not have any remedy before it. Despite holding so, it went on to adjudicate upon the merits of the challenge to determine whether the publication fell foul of Section 4 of the Press Act or not. For that, it held that even though the provision was a combination of Sections 124A and 153A of the IPC, it was different as the element of intention did not come into Section 4 of the Press Act. Though it allowed for criticism of measures of the government, such exemption was subject to the publication not exciting hatred or contempt against the government. The Court quoted James Stephen stating, 'An intention is not seditious if the object is to show that the King has been misled or mistaken in his measures or to point out errors and defects in the Government or constitution with a view to their reformation or to excite the subjects to attempt by lawful means the alteration of any matter in Church or State or to point out with a view to the removal matters which are producing or have a tendency to produce feelings of hatred or ill-will between classes of the subjects.'[40]

The advocate general, on instructions from the government, had conceded that the advocacy of Home Rule was absolutely valid and legal, which the court agreed with as well. It also did not find anything in the articles in question which would suggest that the newspaper wanted India to sever its ties with the British Empire. The court did not spot any element of disloyalty in the publications. It eventually found that there was largely no wilful attempt on the part of Annie Besant to disseminate disaffection or hatred against the government or to create hatred between classes. However, the court pronounced three separate judgments which were unanimous in holding that certain articles appeared to fall foul of the Press Act and could be called seditious. Therefore, it dismissed the challenge and upheld the validity of actions taken by the government under the Press Act.[41]

The very next year, on 16 June 1917, Annie Besant and some of her associates were imprisoned by the government without charge or trial, a move which caused political ripples across India. Leaders who were earlier doubtful about the Home Rule League and reluctant to get involved joined it. People like Jinnah, Tej Bahadur Sapru and Motilal Nehru not only joined the league but also took up leadership positions.

Jawaharlal Nehru, who was already a part of the league, said, 'Mrs Besant's internment also resulted in my father and other moderate leaders joining the Home Rule League . . . My father became the president of the Allahabad branch . . . The adoption by the Congress at Lucknow in 1916 of the Joint Congress-League scheme . . . pleased him greatly as it opened the way to a joint effort, and he was prepared to go ahead then even at the cost of breaking up with his old colleagues of the moderate group.'

Mahatma Gandhi, who disapproved of the movement at that time, wrote a letter to the viceroy on 10 July saying, 'In my humble opinion the internments are a big blunder. Madras was absolutely calm before then, now it is badly disturbed. India as a whole had not made common cause with Mrs Besant, but now she is in a fair way towards commanding India's identity with her methods . . . I myself do not like much in Mrs Besant's methods. I have not liked the idea of political propaganda being carried out during the war. In my opinion our restraint will have been the best propaganda . . . The Congress was trying to capture Mrs Besant. The latter was trying to catch the former. Now they have almost become one.'[42]

While Gandhi himself did not approve of the Home Rule League, what he said in the letter captures the political mood of the country at that time. Eventually, he also converted and supported league propaganda. The British government had created a monster. The political fallout and pressure from the US forced the government to release Besant after just three months, but the damage had been done.[43]

Now, considering the prevailing political environment, there was a lot of suspicion about the Rowlatt Committee as it was seen to be pro-government. When the report was submitted on 15 April 1918, it was met with fierce backlash as every suspicion stood confirmed. The punitive and preventive measures recommended by the Rowlatt Committee were draconian in nature. The Montague–Chelmsford reforms which provided Indians nominal representation in government were contemporaneous with the publication of the Rowlatt Committee Report. The timing gave rise to the feeling that the committee was set up by the British establishment in India as a reaction to the reforms which had originated from the British Parliament and culminated in the enactment of the Government of India Act, 1919. The Act provided for central and provincial legislative assemblies with limited representation and franchise granted to Indians.[44]

The suggestions made by the Rowlatt Committee were accepted and enacted in the form of the Anarchical and Revolutionary Crimes Act, 1919, which was commonly called the Rowlatt Act and derisively called the Black Act. The Rowlatt Act was passed by the Legislative Council of India on 18 March 1919 despite facing vociferous opposition from the non-official (read Indian) members of the council.[45] When the Act was under consideration in the form of a bill, it was opposed along the length and breadth of the country. Surendranath Banerjee, who also opposed the bill in the Legislative Council, was of the view that it had been introduced because of the fear of the European community in India that they would lose their privileged status due to the Montague–Chelmsford reforms.[46]

The Rowlatt Act was a de facto extension of the wartime Defence of India Act that provided for emergency preventive and punitive provisions. The First World War ended in 1919, thus terminating the Defence of India Act. So the British establishment took cover under the Rowlatt Act to continue emergency measures, as described above, to ostensibly counter sedition and 'revolutionary crimes'. However, the provisions were so wide that the government was empowered to use the Act for any political activity opposed to the government by calling it a revolutionary crime. The Act did away with committal proceedings, gave no right of appeal, and accused persons were not even provided legal representation.

Mahatma Gandhi called for a nationwide civil disobedience movement in the form of passive resistance or satyagraha in opposition to the Act.[47] The year 1919 proved to be a watershed year for Gandhi who had only returned to India in 1915 from South Africa. His call for satyagraha was met with support from across the country which observed a strike or hartal from 30 March onwards. He eventually called off the movement due to reports of occurrence of violent activities.

Punjab at this time was under martial law and facing the brunt of British repressive tactics. The Rowlatt Act satyagraha was in full flow in Punjab with strikes and public protests taking place across the state. During this time, on 13 April 1919, occurred one of the greatest massacres in Indian history. The British army under General Dyer without warning opened fire on thousands of people who were holding a peaceful public meeting in Amritsar at Jallianwala Bagh, a park walled from three sides. Hundreds of men, women and children fell victim to the 1650 rounds of bullets on a day when the festival of Baisakhi was being celebrated in Punjab. Thousands were maimed or injured.

During the inquiry into the massacre, Dyer justified it by considering the incident as containing the least amount of firing which would produce the necessary moral and widespread effect![48] Winston Churchill considered General Dyer's actions as 'monstrous'. He said, '. . . one tremendous fact stands out—I mean the slaughter of nearly 400 persons and the wounding of probably three or four times as many, at the Jallian Wallah Bagh on 13th April. That is an episode which appears to me to be without precedent or parallel in the modern history of the British Empire. It is an event of an entirely different order from any of those tragical occurrences which take place when troops are brought into collision with the civil population. It is an extraordinary event, a monstrous event, an event which stands in singular and sinister isolation.'[49]

On the same day as the massacre, the British government claimed that a state of open rebellion against the authority of the government existed in the districts of Lahore and Amritsar. Therefore, it suspended the functions of the ordinary criminal courts within those districts as regards the trial of persons who were openly hostile to the British government, were in armed opposition to its authority, had committed an act of rebellion, or openly aided and abetted the enemies of the British government within those districts. The very next day, the government issued Martial Law Ordinance No. 1 of 1919 which established a three-member commission to try such offences in a manner similar to a summary court martial. For good measure, on 18 April the government also issued a Martial Law (Seditious) Ordinance to cover Section 124A of the IPC. These ordinances were subsequently extended to other districts of Punjab and their application later extended to cover all revolutionary crimes committed after 30 March that year.[50]

The first prominent victim of the martial law ordinance was Lala Harkishen Lal, barrister-at-law, a respected industrialist and a co-founder of Punjab National Bank. He was accused of instigating agitation against the Rowlatt Act in Lahore, where he issued a notice in the local papers calling for the closure of all shops in the district on 6 April 1919. Even though martial law in Punjab was declared only on 13 April, Harkishen Lal was arrested on 11 April and transported to the north-west frontier outside Punjab on the charge of sedition. Later, the martial law ordinances were declared to be retrospective with effect from 30 March, and their application extended even to territories beyond Punjab. Harkishen Lal was again arrested from the north-west frontier on 8 May on charges of sedition, treason, conspiracy to wage war against the government and membership of an unlawful assembly.

He was brought back to Lahore to stand trial before the above-mentioned three-member commission. Lal was denied counsel from outside Punjab even though he had great difficulty in engaging a local lawyer, and eventually sentenced to transportation for life and forfeiture of property. However, his sentence was later commuted to rigorous imprisonment for two years by the government on compassionate grounds.[51]

The unrest in Punjab had claimed lives in Delhi on 30 March 1919, followed by disorder and violence in Lahore on 6 April and 10–12 April. The *Tribune* was a daily newspaper published in Lahore with Kali Nath Roy as its editor. On 6 April and 8–11 April he published articles on the deaths in Delhi with the deceased referred to as martyrs. The newspaper charged the government with grave misconduct in connection with the Punjab unrest. In its issue published on 10 April, it stated that the 'atmosphere was highly surcharged' and the 'public mind in a state of unusual excitement'. Roy was arrested on 6 May and charged with sedition under Section 124A of the IPC. He was tried under martial law and sentenced to two years' rigorous imprisonment by a special tribunal on 28 May.[52]

Roy applied for special leave to appeal against his conviction as there was no right to appeal against judgments of the special commissions set up under the martial law ordinances. He was granted special leave to appeal before the Bombay High Court by the King in Council on 18 August. Roy appealed his conviction on two grounds. First, that his trial by summary court martial was unconstitutional[53] and therefore bad in law; and second, that he was not guilty under Section 124A of the IPC. A bench comprising of five judges of the Bombay High Court dismissed his first ground of appeal at the outset based on a case law[54] which had already held that trial under martial law in Punjab was constitutional. In the earlier case, the Bombay High Court had held that such a trial would have been unconstitutional if the accused were a British subject of the crown. However, that protection did not extend to an Indian subject of the crown.

As to the second ground, the High Court refused to interfere with the finding of the Special Tribunal which had tried Kali Nath Roy. It was of the view that the decision of the tribunal was based on facts which had to be looked at in the context of the local conditions prevailing in Punjab at the time of publication of the offending articles. The High Court refrained from giving its findings on facts as it felt that the special commission would have been in a better position to appreciate whether the intention of the articles was punishable under Section 124A of the Penal Code or not.

Finding no reason to interfere on either ground, the High Court dismissed the appeal filed by Kali Nath Roy.

However, the dismissal was more or less an inconsequential outcome as Roy had in the meantime received a royal pardon. His sentence had been reduced to three months' simple imprisonment along with a fine of Rs 1000 during the pendency of the appeal.

Martial law had initially been introduced in only five districts of Punjab: Lahore, Amritsar, Gujranwala, Gujrat and Lyallpore. On 28 May 1919, it was lifted from the district of Gujrat and by 9 June from the other districts except Lahore. On 11 June, even Lahore was brought out of the shadow of martial law. After the end of this period of martial law in Punjab, all the Special Tribunals were dissolved.[55]

The Special Tribunals had tried 852 persons, out of whom 582 were convicted and 270 acquitted. Offences against martial law orders, that is, orders issued by the General Officer Commanding, which included curfew and price control orders, among others, were considered minor offences. About 1500 such cases were summarily decided either by court martial or by ordinary courts. With regard to the serious cases which included waging war against the Crown, and sedition, sentences imposed by the Special Tribunals were always subject to revision by the government of Punjab as well as by the government of India. In nearly 500 out of the 582 cases of conviction for revolutionary crimes, the government had reduced or commuted the sentences imposed by the Special Tribunals. Further, wherever any sentence of forfeiture of property was imposed by the Special Tribunals, the Punjab government had reversed it without fail. By August 1919, out of the 108 death sentences imposed for revolutionary crimes, only eighteen had been executed. Twenty-eight out of the 108 had been reduced to transportation for life, twenty-three to imprisonment for ten years, thirteen to imprisonment for seven years, and twenty-one to imprisonment for even shorter periods.[56]

7

Gandhi, Azad and Nehru: Politics of Sedition

I would like to state that I entirely endorse the learned Advocate-General's remarks in connection with my humble self. I think that he was entirely fair to me in all statements that he has made, because it is very true and I have no desire whatsoever to conceal from this Court the fact that to preach disaffection towards the existing system of Government has become almost a passion with me. And the Advocate-General is also entirely in the right when he says that my preaching of disaffection did not commence with my connection with 'Young India' but that it commenced much earlier . . . I do not plead any extenuating act. I am here, therefore, to invite and submit to the highest penalty that can be inflicted upon me for what in law is a deliberate crime and what appears to me to be the highest duty of the citizen.[1]

This was what Mahatma Gandhi told the trial court in Ahmedabad on 18 March 1922 before reading out his formal written statement during his trial for sedition. Calling sedition the highest duty of the citizen, he asked the judge to either resign or to inflict the highest penalty possible under Section 124A, if he believed the system of law being enforced by him was good for the people of India.[2]

Before we go to the trial, it is important to understand why the prosecution took place.[3]

In April 1919, Gandhi had called off the satyagraha against the Rowlatt Act as it had led to violence in many parts of the country. Even in the face of the campaign of repression unleashed by the British government, Gandhi dissuaded his associates and followers from holding strikes or demonstrations against the government. He justified his decision by saying:

> We cannot close the shops or suspend business, because that would mean risk of disturbances. Disturbances are not a part of satyagraha. The foundation of satyagraha is based on truth and non-violence . . . We have declared that we will not submit to the Rowlatt Act and that we will disobey other laws. That civil disobedience can only be practiced by one who adheres to truth and non-violence. Without that civil disobedience is foolish and could not help us to achieve anything for the public good.[4]

In an announcement published in *Sanj Vartaman* on 3 May 1919, Mahatma Gandhi announced that he would resume the Satyagraha and Civil Disobedience Movement on 1 July of that year unless the Rowlatt Act was withdrawn by then. He intended to extend the movement to Punjab, which was under repressive martial law and was still reeling from the horrors of Jallianwala Bagh. He exhorted the need to refrain from violence or rioting during the movement. The British government was convinced that Mahatma Gandhi had assumed absolute leadership of the 'satyagraha sabha', which they considered to be a secret society whose objective was to break laws and excite anti-government feelings in order to make governance of India impossible.

Ironically, the Rowlatt Act, the campaign against which brought Mahatma Gandhi to the forefront of the freedom movement in India, remained a non-starter and was effectively a dormant legislation which was never invoked. On 21 July 1919, Gandhi called off the Civil Disobedience Movement 'on account of indication of goodwill on the part of the Government and advice from many of his friends'.[5]

This period was followed by the Khilafat Movement by Indian Muslims against the British government in 1920 (whose seeds were sown in 1919 itself). The movement had resulted from the defeat of Turkey at the hands of the British army in the Second World War. Turkey was dispossessed of its lands and the Ottoman sultan of Turkey placed under the control of the allied powers led by the British. Therefore, the allies became the real rulers of Turkey with the sultan reduced to a figurehead. This caused great resentment amongst Indian Muslims as they saw it as an attack against Islam because the sultan was considered the caliph of Islam. Gandhi backed the movement to the hilt as he saw it as a vehicle to unite Hindus and Muslims. He combined the Khilafat Movement led by the Ali brothers with his non-cooperation movement to create a bigger and better weapon against the British government. The non-cooperation movement involved giving up honorary posts, titles and government posts, including police and military jobs, and refusing to pay taxes. Though the government considered the movement unconstitutional, it was wary of prosecuting the people involved in the movement. It was also mistaken in its belief that the non-cooperation movement would dwindle on its own.[6]

The government, however, came out of its misbelief at the time of the visit of the Prince of Wales on Christmas Eve in 1921. The visit was opposed through the observation of protest meetings and strikes across India, some of which turned violent. The government reacted with repressive measures like the re-introduction of the Seditious Meetings Act across Punjab, Bihar, Bengal, Assam and Burma. The government took on the civil disobedience and non-cooperation juggernaut with its full might and restricted the freedom of speech and association. In early 1922, Mahatma Gandhi gave an ultimatum to the British government. He referred to the government's assault on innocent people, harsh treatment of prisoners, and suppression of freedom of speech, freedom of press and freedom of association. He called mass civil disobedience an 'imperative duty' in the face of the repressive policies of the government. He asked the government to revise its policy and set free political prisoners convicted of non-violent crimes, failing which he announced a campaign of mass civil disobedience to be launched from Bardoli in Gujarat. The government rejected his demands, thereby laying the ground for a pan-Indian, non-violent Civil Disobedience Movement. The entire nation was galvanized and preparations made across all the presidencies and provinces. No one realized that their preparations would be in vain.[7]

The events of 5 February 1922 ensured that the movement would be stillborn. A procession in a village named Chauri Chaura in the United Provinces was fired upon by police officers who shut themselves inside a police station to escape mob fury once they ran out of ammunition.

The mob, however, did not relent and set the police station on fire. The officers, in their attempt to escape the blaze, were captured by the rampaging mob. Twenty-two persons were hacked to death and their bodies burnt in the blaze. The event sent shock waves across the nation. As collateral damage, Mahatma Gandhi called off the Civil Disobedience and Non-cooperation Movements indefinitely. While the Chauri Chaura incident was condemned by all, most Indians felt aggrieved by the withdrawal and suspension of the nationwide campaign. Without passing judgment on Gandhi's decision, it is safe to say that his popularity suffered a major downward spiral due to his retreat.[8]

The government considered it an opportune moment to arrest Gandhi, something which it had not done during the movement for fear of mass reprisals. But they were emboldened by his loss of popularity and support and arrested him in Ahmedabad on 10 March 1922.[9]

The complete record and detailed account of Gandhi's trial for sedition under Section 124A of the IPC is contained in *Trial of Gandhiji*, published by the registrar of the Gujarat High Court at Ahmedabad in 1965.

Gandhi was the editor and publisher of a weekly journal named *Young India* which he had founded in 1919. His arrest was the result of four articles published in *Young India*, namely 'Disaffection a Virtue',[10] 'Tampering with Loyalty',[11] 'The Puzzle and Its Solution'[12] and 'Shaking the Manes'.[13] The sanction for his arrest was issued on 4 March 1922 by the secretary to the government of Bombay (Home Department), which also included the sanction to arrest Shankarlal Banker, who was the proprietor of *Young India*. Banker was arrested a day before Gandhi's arrest. Though the sanction for prosecution under Section 124A was issued with respect to four articles, the actual prosecution focused on three articles, with 'Disaffection a Virtue' being left out.

The first article, 'Tampering with Loyalty', had supported the Khilafat Movement and reiterated the call to Indian sepoys to quit serving in the British army. Gandhi wrote that sedition had become the creed of the Congress and every non-cooperator was pledged to preach disaffection towards the government established by law. He further said that non-cooperation deliberately aimed at the overthrow of the government and was therefore legally seditious in terms of the IPC.

Both Gandhi and Banker pleaded guilty to the charge of promoting sedition before the Sessions Court of Ahmedabad and refused to call any witness in their defence. The Sessions Court, presided over by Judge R.S. Broomfield, conducted their trial on 18 March 1922. Sir J.T. Strangman, the advocate general, contended that the offending articles were part of an organized campaign harmful to the government.

Strangman had wanted a full trial against both the accused but the judge disagreed with him because of the guilty plea submitted by them. He felt that examination of evidence would be unnecessary, but he was prepared to hear out the prosecution as well as the accused. Neither Gandhi nor Banker had engaged any lawyer and were representing themselves before the court.

The prosecution had contended that since Gandhi was a highly educated individual and a recognized leader, the harm caused by his writings was considerably higher. Strangman referred to occurrences in Bombay, Madras and Chauri Chaura which led to murder and destruction of property. He pointed out that even though the articles impressed upon the practice of non-violence, the effect of preaching disaffection was contrary to it. Mahatma Gandhi responded by endorsing what Strangman had said and admitted that preaching disaffection had become a passion with him. He accepted the blame for the crimes of violence committed in Bombay, Madras and elsewhere and said, 'I wish to endorse all the blame that the learned Advocate General has thrown on my shoulders in connection with the Bombay occurrences, Madras occurrences and the Chauri Chaura occurrences. Thinking over these deeply and sleeping over them night after night, it is impossible for me to dissociate myself from the diabolical crimes of Chauri Chaura or the mad outrages of Bombay . . . I should have known that I was playing with fire. I ran the risk, and if I was set free, I would still do the same.'

He then read out a written statement to explain how he had turned from being a British loyalist and cooperator to an uncompromising 'disaffectionist and a non-cooperator'. He had supported the British Empire in South Africa as well as in India during the First World War despite having felt denigrated by them. The turning point for him came in 1919 with the Rowlatt Act, which was followed by the horrors of Punjab, especially the massacre at Jallianwala Bagh in Amritsar. The third setback was the breaking of promises when it came to the treatment of Turkey at the hands of the British. This spelled the start of the Khilafat Movement, which was wholeheartedly supported by Gandhi. He strongly criticized the bureaucracy and judiciary for having repressed innocent Indians, who always ended up getting the short end of the stick as compared to their British and European fellow citizens.

On the charges against him he said, 'Section 124A, under which I am happily charged, is perhaps the prince among the political sections of the Indian Penal Code designed to suppress the liberty of the citizen. Affection cannot be measured or regulated by law. If one has no affection for a person or system, one should be free to give the fullest expression to his disaffection, so long as he does not contemplate, promote or incite to violence. But the section under which Mr Banker and I are charged is one under which mere promotion of disaffection is a crime. I have studied some of the cases tried under it and I know that some of the most loved of India's patriots have been convicted under it. I consider it a privilege, therefore, to be charged under that section. I have endeavoured to give in their briefest outline the reasons for my disaffection. I have no personal ill-will against any single administrator, much less can I have any disaffection towards the King's person. But I hold it to be a virtue to be disaffected towards a Government which in its totality has done more harm to India than any previous system. India is less manly under the British rule than she ever was before. Holding such a belief, I consider it a sin to have affection for the system. And it has been a precious privilege for me to be able to write what I have in the various articles tendered in evidence against me.'

He thereafter called upon the judge to first consider whether the law of sedition was evil or not, and punish him with the severest penalty if he found that it was not. He called upon the judge to resign and dissociate himself from evil if he found otherwise.

The judge appeared to hold Mahatma Gandhi in high regard and found it difficult to determine the sentence against him. He acknowledged the fact that Gandhi was not an ordinary accused. He was revered by millions for whom he was a leader and a patriot. However, he found it difficult to understand how Gandhi could believe that his political teachings would not amount to violence even though he asked people to refrain from it. He felt that violence was the inevitable consequence of Gandhi's message to the masses.

Judge Broomfield invoked the second trial of Bal Gangadhar Tilak under Section 124A of the IPC and proposed to pass a similar sentence as the nature of both trials was similar. He therefore imposed an identical sentence of six years' simple imprisonment; two years for each article. He, however, hoped that the government would reduce the sentence in the future. Shankarlal Banker was sentenced to one year's simple imprisonment—six months each for the first two articles—and a fine of Rs 1000 for the third article. Failing the payment of the fine, Banker was to serve an additional six months' simple imprisonment.

Gandhi thanked the judge for associating his name with that of Bal Gangadhar Tilak and stated that the sentence was more lenient than he had expected. Banker and Gandhi were then taken to serve out their sentence at Sabarmati Jail in Ahmedabad, which marked the end of the hundred-minute trial![14]

Judge Broomfield's wish came true as the government of Bombay reduced Gandhi's sentence and ordered his release on 4 February 1924, which was carried out the next day at Yeravada Central Prison in Poona where he was serving his sentence by then.

As collateral damage, Gandhi's conviction resulted in him losing his place as a barrister with Inner Temple in London. It removed him from its roll of barristers and disbarred him from practising law.[15] Not that Mahatma Gandhi was looking at a career in law, but the collateral damage was remarkable, nonetheless.

At about the same time, another leading light of the Khilafat and Non-cooperation Movements, Maulana Abul Kalam Azad, was arrested in Calcutta in December 1921 before the arrival of the prince of Wales. Maulana Azad was charged with sedition under Section 124A of the Code for a couple of speeches he had delivered in July 1921. He was tried before the presidency magistrate in Calcutta within the jail premises itself. Like Gandhi and Banker, even Azad refused to defend himself and pled guilty to the charge of sedition and was duly sentenced on 9 February 1922 to one year's rigorous imprisonment.[16]

Azad felt that the sentence was too light for him. Prior to his conviction he read out a written statement running into thirty pages, which Gandhi called '. . . an eloquent thesis giving the Maulana's view on Khilafat and nationalism . . . an oration deserving penal servitude for life'. In his statement, Azad claimed to have descended from a long line of satyagrahis starting from Jesus. Talking about sedition, he said, '. . . nothing can be a higher crime against the domination of Government, as at present established, than the agitation which seeks to terminate its unlimited authority in the name of liberty and justice. I fully admit that I am not only guilty of such agitation, but that I belong to that band of pioneers who originally sowed the seed of such agitation in the heart of our nation and dedicated their whole lives to the cherishing and breeding of this holy discontent.'[17]

The start of the next decade saw another wave of civil disobedience, which had its roots in the *purna swaraj* (complete independence) declaration of the Indian National Congress on 31 December 1929. The All India Congress Committee even decided to mark 26 January as Independence Day! Civil disobedience included non-payment of taxes and a demand for removal of the salt tax which was repressive for the poor sections of society. In March 1930, Mahatma Gandhi embarked on a historic march to Dandi in coastal Gujarat, from his ashram in Sabarmati, to break the law prohibiting the indigenous manufacturing of salt. The march was an era-defining event and was the real birth of that phase of civil disobedience. In October 1930, Jawaharlal Nehru, fresh from his release from prison after serving a sentence for breaking salt laws, called for a no-tax campaign at a meeting of the United Provinces Congress Committee. He called upon landlords and peasants alike to participate in the campaign.[18]

On 12 October, while addressing a large gathering, Nehru said:

> We have adopted the policy of nonviolence because we believe in it and wish to give it the fullest trial in all honesty . . . The first phase of the great struggle has come to an end. It has been marked by a national awakening to which the world has been an admiring witness. Now the second stage is beginning, the stage of our laying the foundations of a future, free India. Every city, every mohalla, every village must now play its part in this effort by making itself ready to become a living, self-dependent entity in free India. We must be prepared not only to pay any taxes to the British Government but also to do without any service which they may render to us.[19]

Thereafter, Nehru was forbidden to speak in public by the police, but he defied orders and addressed a mass gathering of peasants at Allahabad on 19 October and decided to start the no-tax campaign from Allahabad itself. However, before he could even reach home from the rally, he was arrested for sedition and taken to prison.

In the true spirit of non-cooperation, even Nehru refused to defend himself and pleaded guilty to the charge under Section 124A of the IPC. In his statement to the magistrate, he said, 'There can be no compromise between freedom and slavery, and between truth and falsehood. We realized that the price of freedom is blood and suffering—the blood of our own countrymen and the suffering of the noblest in the land—and that price we shall pay in full measure . . . To the Indian people I cannot express my gratitude sufficiently for their confidence and affection. It has been the greatest joy in my life to serve in this glorious struggle and to do my little bit for the cause. I pray that my countrymen and countrywomen will carry on the good fight unceasingly till success crowns their effort and we realise the India of our dreams.' On 24 October 1930, he was sentenced to two years in prison for sedition under Section 124A and for breaking other laws. However, he was released after serving ninety-seven days.[20]

Nehru's second tryst with sedition was to occur three years after his release from prison after his first conviction for sedition. In January 1934, Nehru travelled to Calcutta in solidarity with the repressed masses of Bengal. During his four-day stay there, he had addressed some meetings, out of which three speeches formed the basis of the sedition charge against him.[21]

The first speech was delivered at Albert Hall in Calcutta on 17 January on 'The Character of the National Struggle'. After apprising the gathering of the nationalist movements across India, Nehru criticized the British government for the brutal, disgusting and vulgar mentality with which it was governing India. He said:

> It is an extraordinary vulgarity of imperialism. Why is that so? Because imperialism of today, in spite of the strength that it seems to possess, is in a tottering condition, and when a great system like this totters, when it is afraid of failing, then it loses all control, its culture and education and everything else goes. It becomes vulgar and it becomes abusive . . . these are the signs of a decadent system. The system is utterly decadent. Therefore you find utter cruelty, utter vandalism. That is what is happening specially in Bengal and

the Frontier Province . . . Therefore, do not expect anything from appeals to chivalry or appeals to justice or the like. We are today in the midst of a historic struggle, which all nations have to face at a particular time and from that there is only one escape—victory of one side or the other. I hope you will realise that and work for that.[22]

The next speech was also delivered at Albert Hall the very next day on 'The Futility of Terrorism and the Nature of Mass Movement'. As the title suggests, Nehru was critical of terrorism as a form of nationalist movement and called it weak, futile, harmful and completely out of date. However, he preached disloyalty and said:

In the Congress we have nothing to do with loyalty. We are disloyal . . . and it is our business to preach disloyalty . . . Are you going to be loyal to those people who humiliate your people, who degrade your country, or are you going to be loyal to your own country, to your own people? . . . Indian nationalism and British imperialism are at close grips with each other. British imperialism may succeed in suppressing Indian nationalism, but remember this also: that while Indian nationalism will grow again, but British imperialism will be suppressed once for all by Indian nationalism [23]

The third speech was delivered in Hindi at Maheshwari Bhawan on 18 January. However, according to Nehru, the translation of the speech was grossly inaccurate, conveyed the wrong impression and misrepresented what he had actually said. The speech has not been published in Nehru's selected works for this same reason.[24]

Nehru was arrested from Allahabad on 12 February on warrants issued by the Calcutta police. He was produced before the chief presidency magistrate on 13 February, who charged him with sedition under Section 124A and offered to hold the trial in private to protect Nehru's feelings!

Nehru refused the offer and conveyed his preference of being tried in public. His trial was held on 15 February before the chief presidency magistrate. He refused to take part in the proceedings, just like his earlier sedition trial, and did not enter any defence, thereby pleading guilty. He admitted that his activities had been seditious for years, that is, if sedition meant the desire to achieve the independence of India and put an end to foreign domination. He further admitted having attempted to put an end to British rule in India and therefore being guilty of sedition. He condemned the British government in Bengal and its brutalities. He concluded his statement by saying, 'It is a terrible thing when brutality becomes a method of behaviour.'[25]

Thanks to his guilty plea, Nehru was sentenced to two years' simple imprisonment under Section 124A of the IPC on 16 February 1934. In fact, Sushil Kumar Sinha, who was the chief presidency magistrate, felt regret for the trial and conviction and thought Nehru would be wasted in prison. He suggested that if Nehru would express some form of regret, he could put an end to the matter and save himself from incarceration. He offered to adjourn the sentencing hearing and also offered to see the governor himself to speak on behalf of Nehru. Though moved by the earnestness of the gesture, Nehru refused to show any remorse or regret. He felt that any such move would result in a win for the government. Therefore, Sinha was forced to impose the sentence of two years' imprisonment.[26]

Again, Nehru did not have to serve the full sentence but was released after serving 565 days. The remainder of the sentence was suspended by the government on compassionate grounds as his wife, Kamala Nehru, was seriously ill.[27]

PART III

SEDITION IN THE REPUBLIC

8

No Love Lost: 'Sedition' in the Constituent Assembly

On 22 November 1934, a gentleman by the name of Kamal Krishna Sircar delivered a speech at Shradhanand Park in Calcutta. It was a meeting of the Bengal Youth League, a communist group. Naturally, the meeting had a red banner with the hammer, sickle and star signage on it. It was attended by young Bengali students and featured a number of speeches. At this meeting, Sircar moved a resolution condemning the outlawing of the Communist Party of India and various other trade and labour associations. He attributed capitalist motives to the government's decision to ban various communist organizations, and even called Gandhi and the Congress government stooges. All in all, the speech recommended the communist form of government over the capitalist one and called upon young Bengali students to join the Bengal Youth League to propagate communism.[1]

Unfortunately for Sircar, the government saw red.

Sircar was charged with sedition under Section 124A of the IPC and convicted to serve one year's rigorous imprisonment. Upon an appeal being filed, a two-judge bench of the Calcutta High Court set aside his conviction. It found it absurd to say that such a speech would amount to sedition. It was of the view that if such speeches were considered seditious then every argument for one form of government over the present form would amount to hatred of the government and bring it into contempt. The court felt that the magistrate did not like communism, and neither did the High Court, but it deemed that feeling irrelevant for the purpose of a trial under Section 124A. It did not find such dislike of an ideology to be good reason to hold someone guilty of sedition. Holding that the right to free speech existed in India, unlike other countries, the court did not find it wise to institute sedition prosecutions against speeches of the kind delivered by Kamal Krishna Sircar. It accordingly acquitted him of the sedition charge.[2]

Even earlier, the Calcutta High Court had held that in a charge under Section 124A of the IPC, the prosecution must prove to the hilt that the intention of the writer or the speaker, as it may be, was to bring or attempt to bring into hatred or contempt or attempt to excite disaffection towards the government established by law in British India. The essence of the crime of sedition was to be found in the intention of the accused. The prosecution, therefore, had to establish that the intention of the accused was exactly as what is defined in the section, and mere tendency to promote such a feeling was not sufficient to justify a conviction.[3]

However, the intention of the writer or the speaker had to be gathered from the particular language used in the offending article or speech. Basically, what needed to be seen was whether the meaning of a writing or speech, as understood by people to whom the same was addressed, was seditious or not. In fact, it was not open to the speaker or writer accused of sedition to contend that he or she did not intend their language to bear the meaning which it would naturally or literally mean.[4] Basically, it follows the principle that people are assumed to intend the natural and reasonable consequences of their actions. This was consistent with Justice Strachey's view that if hatred or contempt against the government was caused or disaffection excited, then whether the accused intended to commit sedition or not was irrelevant. Therefore, under Section 124A, if the article or speech in question excites or attempts to excite hatred, contempt or disaffection towards the government, then it is assumed that the accused intended to do so in fact.

In ascertaining intention, as explained above, it was important to read any offending article or speech as a whole in a 'fair, free and liberal spirit'. The Calcutta High Court said:

> . . . one should not pause upon an objectionable sentence here, or a strong word there, but that the article as a whole should be dealt with in a spirit of freedom and should not be viewed with an eye of narrow and fastidious criticism but, as has been said in another case, should be viewed in a free, bold, manly and generous spirit towards the accused. As we read the cases to which our attention was drawn during the course of the argument, the expression in the section 'calculated to bring into hatred or contempt or excite or attempt to excite disaffection' must, as a rule of construction, be very narrowly construed so as to interfere as little as possible with the liberty of the subject and the freedom of speech.[5]

Another aspect of Section 124A is that seditious activity must be directed against the 'government established by law' for it to be an offence. As noted above in the *Kamal*

Krishna Sircar case, merely an attack on a particular form of government over the prevailing form would not amount to sedition. The Calcutta High Court in 1932 held that a government established by law would refer to persons authorized by law to administer executive government in any part of British India, collectively as a body and not as individuals.[6] Since the government established by law would be distinct from individuals who may be administering the government, even strong criticism of ministers accusing them of inefficiency, corruption or personal animosity would not tend to excite hatred, contempt or disaffection towards the government as a whole.[7] However, it is not necessary to constitute an offence of sedition that the target of such activity be the structure or framework of the government. It was sufficient to show that the target of seditious activities was a body of persons carrying out executive functions for the government, like a provincial or local government.[8] Even if seditious activity was not directed against the government in explicit language but the inference was necessary by implication, it amounted to sedition under Section 124A.

The position of the law regarding sedition was consistent until 1942 during the Second World War. The viceroy had issued a proclamation of emergency as the government feared that the security of India was threatened, both externally and internally. The Defence of India Act was in place since 1939 granting emergency powers to the government, similar to what existed during the First World War, as discussed earlier. According to the Rules promulgated under the Act, every person was prohibited from bringing into hatred or contempt, or to excite disaffection towards 'His Majesty or the Crown representative or the Government established by law in British India or in any other part of His Majesty's dominions'.[9]

In *Niharendu Dutt Majumdar v. The King Emperor*,[10] a three-judge bench led by Chief Justice Maurice Gwyer of the Federal Court, the predecessor of the Supreme Court of India, noted that the above-mentioned prohibition contained language identical to Section 124A of the IPC. Even though the Rule did not contain explanations as provided in Section 124A, the Court felt that doing so was unnecessary. It was of the view that the explanations should be read into the Rule while interpreting the relevant rule under the Defence of India Rules. Having done so, the Federal Court held:

> The time is long past when mere criticism of governments was sufficient to constitute sedition, for it is recognized that the right to utter honest and reasonable criticism is a source of strength to a community than a weakness. Criticism of an existing system of government is not excluded, nor even the expression for desire for a different system altogether. The language of section 124A of the Penal Code, if read literally even with the explanations attached to it, would suffice to make a surprising number of persons in this country guilty of sedition; but no one supposes that it is to be read in this literal sense.

The Federal Court pointed out that the language of Section 124A is derived from English law but the system of trial in England was different from that in India. In England, such cases were tried by a jury, which acted as a check on the extravagant interpretations given by judges or the legislature. Therefore, it was of the opinion that in India judges must place themselves in the position of a jury and look at every sedition trial with a broad view in order to apply general principles of the law of sedition on a case-to-case basis. In order to arrive at the general principles, the Federal Court relied upon Justice Fitzgerald's findings in *Reg v. Sullivan*[11] wherein he enunciated that, 'Sedition . . . embraces all those practices, whether by word, deed or writing, which are calculated to disturb the tranquillity of the State and lead ignorant persons to subvert the Government. The objects of sedition generally are to induce discontent and insurrection, to stir up opposition to the Government, and to bring the administration of justice into contempt; and the very tendency of sedition is to incite the people to insurrection and rebellion.'

He further said that, 'Sedition has been described as disloyalty in action, and the law considers as sedition all those practices which have for their object to excite discontent or disaffection, to create public disturbance, or to lead to civil war; to bring into hatred or contempt the sovereign or Government, the laws or the constitution of the realm and generally all endeavours to promote public disorder.'

The Federal Court was of the view that the above findings accurately stated the law of sedition, as they were based on the study of a large number of judicial pronouncements under English law. It stated that sedition was not made an offence merely to tend to the injured vanity of the government. It was made an offence to take care of situations where its citizens stop respecting or obeying the law, thus leading to anarchy.

In the words of the Federal Court, the broad principles of sedition as an offence against the State were, 'Public disorder, or the reasonable anticipation or likelihood of public disorder, is thus the gist of the offence. The acts or words complained of must either incite disorder or must be such as to satisfy reasonable men that that is their intention or tendency.' It felt that the judiciary's duty was to maintain a balance between the government and the rights of its citizens to have freedom of speech.

The position of law as enunciated by the Federal Court was short-lived. It was called into question before the Privy Council in England in 1947 in the case of *King Emperor v. Sadashiv Narayan Bhalerao*[12] before a bench of five councillors led by Lord William Thankerton.

The Privy Council refused to accept the principle and test of sedition laid down by the Federal Court of India in the *Niharendu Dutt* case. It found that the word 'sedition' did not occur in Section 124A of the IPC but was only found in the marginal note of the legislation. Consequently, it held that the marginal note just lent its name to the provision and was not in itself an operative part of Section 124A. Therefore, the Federal Court's restriction of the provisions of Section 124A was not justified by the marginal note. English common law and judgments were held to be inapplicable to Section 124A as sedition was explicitly defined in the provision, as opposed to being undefined under the common law.

Therefore, the Privy Council held that the element of incitement of disorder read into Section 124A by the Federal Court was incorrect, just like the test that reasonable men must be satisfied of such intention or tendency. It reinstated the principle laid down by Justice Strachey in Tilak's first sedition trial, which was subsequently approved by the Privy Council. Justice Strachey had given a very wide meaning to the word 'disaffection' contained in Section 124A to include a mere lack of affection and a feeling which did not translate into an overt act of hatred, enmity, dislike, hostility, contempt or any other form of ill-will against the government. He held that 'disloyalty' was the best term to describe 'disaffection' as it comprehended every possible form of bad feeling against the Government. He explicitly held that causing mutiny or the likelihood of causing mutiny, rebellion or any kind of disturbance was irrelevant for the purpose of interpretation of the provision.[13]

Basically, the Privy Council set aside the decision of the Federal Court in the *Niharendu Dutt* case and reinstated the principle that incitement to violence was not a necessary ingredient for the offence of sedition as defined in Section 124A of the IPC.

This decision was pronounced on 18 February 1947. India became independent in just under six months thereafter.

One would think that the Indian masses, and its political class, repressed by the law of sedition and other similar laws, would burn them at the stake upon having rid themselves of the British.

Unfortunately, this was not to be.

India became independent on 15 August 1947 after the creation of the separate state of Pakistan one day prior. The partition was preceded, and succeeded, by bloodshed and communal conflict. While political manoeuvres between the Congress, Muslim League and the British government were ongoing, the country went through major communal strife, especially in Bengal, Assam and Punjab. Prior to Partition, elections were held for the establishment of an interim government in India to facilitate the transition to independence, as well as for the creation of the Constituent Assembly for the drafting of the Constitution of India.[14]

Though the Muslim League participated in the interim government, they desisted from participation in the Constituent Assembly which met for the first time on 9 December 1946. The British government's earlier plan was to transfer power in (undivided) India by June 1948, but it had to be accelerated in view of the breakdown of relations and negotiations between the Congress and the Muslim League which made Partition an inevitability. A separate Constituent Assembly for Pakistan was elected in June 1947 by the regions which were slated to become Pakistan, and the members of the Constituent Assembly of India from such regions ceased to be so.

On 18 July 1947, the British Parliament enacted the Indian Independence Act for the creation of two separate dominions of India and Pakistan (including East Pakistan) and to provide for other consequential matters. The Act fixed 15 August 1947 as the 'appointed day' for setting up the two countries. East Bengal and West Punjab were carved out and included in Pakistan, with Baluchistan, the North-West Frontier Province and Sind going to Pakistan in their entirety. However, the Act did not prevent the accession of Indian states to either India or Pakistan. This would lead to a lot of strife within India later.

The legislatures of both new dominions were given full power to frame laws for their respective countries and the Constituent Assemblies empowered to draft the new constitutions. The Constituent Assemblies were tasked with the role of being the first legislatures of the two countries.

The Fundamental Rights Sub-Committee of the Constituent Assembly, headed by Sardar Vallabhbhai Patel, placed a draft interim report on fundamental rights before the Assembly for its consideration on 29 April 1947.[15] In response to the interim report, Somnath Lahiri, who was the sole representative of the Communist Party of India, remarked that the fundamental rights had been framed from the point of view of a police constable. The reason for such consternation was that almost all such rights had been subjected to provisos (clauses which restrict the main clause) which took away the right completely in 'grave emergency'.[16]

He pointed out that Indians had suffered in the past due to denial of rights by an 'alien and autocratic government' which restricted the liberty of the press. Therefore, he felt it necessary that the press in free India should be free of restrictions and protected by the Constitution. He remarked that the provisions sought to be brought in would leave Indians worse off than earlier. He made a special mention of restriction of seditious speech by contending, 'Here according to Patel a seditious speech is a punishable crime. If I say at any time in the future, or the Socialist Party says, that the Government in power is despicable, Sardar Patel if he is in power at that time, will be able to put the Socialist Party people and myself in jail, though as far as I know, even in England a speech, however seditious it may be, is never considered a crime unless an overt act is done.'

Lahiri was not done yet. He attacked an amendment proposed by C. Rajagopalachari which wanted to make the restriction more stringent. He said, 'These are the fundamental bases of the fundamental rights of a free country, but here a seditious speech is going to be an offence; and Shri Rajagopalachari wants to go further. Sardar Patel would punish us if we make a speech, but Rajaji would punish us even before we have made the speech. He wants to prevent the making of the speech itself if in his great wisdom he thinks that the fellow is going to make a seditious speech.'

He concluded his objection by asserting that the political opposition must have full freedom to express its views for democracy to develop.

The severe opposition mounted by Somnath Lahiri proved to be effective as Sardar Patel deleted the word 'seditious' from the proviso to Clause 8, which granted liberty for the exercise of freedom of speech.[17]

After much debate, the draft Constitution of India was tabled before the Assembly on 21 February 1948. Fundamental rights were enumerated under Chapter III of the draft Constitution with Article 13 providing for 'protection of certain rights including freedom of speech, etc.'. Article 13(1)(a) guaranteed all citizens the right to freedom of speech and expression. However, Article 13(2) provided that such freedom of speech and expression would not affect any existing law or prevent the State from making any law relating to 'libel, slander, defamation, sedition or any other matter which offends against decency or morality or undermines the authority or foundation of the State'. Sedition found its way back as a restriction of freedom of speech and, as Gautam Bhatia[18] points out, restrictions on the right to freedom of speech and expression were not qualified by the word 'reasonable', thereby potentially empowering the government to draft sweeping legislations to curb free speech.

The debate on Article 13 commenced on 1 December 1948 with Damodar Swarup Seth[19] suggesting an amendment which proposed absolute freedom of speech with no riders and added the freedom of press as a right distinct from freedom of speech and expression. He was of the view that Article 13 in its original form cancelled out the rights guaranteed under it by placing onerous restrictions. He pointed out that the restrictions to freedom of speech and expression were couched in very broad terms, which would ensure that the Indian press would not have any greater freedom than what existed under British rule. He was of the view that even citizens would have no means of getting the law against sedition invalidated despite the same having the potential to violate their civil rights.[20]

Thereafter, K.M. Munshi[21] proposed an amendment to Article 13 whereby he sought to remove the word 'sedition' from the list of restrictions to free speech while retaining restrictions on libel, slander and defamation. He also proposed to substitute the words 'undermines the authority or foundation of the State' with the words 'undermines the security of, or tends to overthrow the State'. He said, 'The importance of this amendment is that it seeks to delete the word "sedition" and uses much better phraseology . . . The object is to remove the word "sedition" which is of doubtful and varying import and to introduce words which are now considered to be the gist of an offence against the State'.

He quoted the judgment of the Federal Court in the *Niharendu Dutt Majumdar* case to underline that criticism of the government is the essence of democracy. He demanded that a distinction be drawn between criticism of the government and incitement of which would undermine the security or order on which civilized life is based. He advocated that Justice Gwyer's interpretation of Section 124A of the IPC better reflected the evolution of Indian society and anything contrary to that would be bad law.

Sardar Hukum Singh, a representative from East Punjab, went one step ahead and proposed that all the restrictive clauses of Article 13 should be done away with. He felt that the fundamental freedoms granted under Article 13 would be left at the mercy of the State machinery if the restrictions were not removed. He was followed by Thakur Das Bhargava, another representative from that region, who proposed that restrictions on free speech should be preceded by the word 'reasonable', and the word 'sedition' be deleted altogether. By suggesting the insertion of the word 'reasonable', Bhargava was trying to put a soul in the lifeless Article 13. He was of the view that if the word 'reasonable' was inserted, then it would leave the door open for courts to see whether the restrictions imposed were reasonable and necessary or not. It would act as a safeguard against executive and legislative overreach and prevent the infringement of freedoms by the government of the day.

When the debate on Article 13 continued the next day, Seth Govind Das[22] mounted an opposition to 'sedition' as a restriction on free speech. It will be worthwhile to reproduce what he had to say about the desirability of 'sedition' in Article 13.

He said:

I find that the first sub-clause refers to freedom of speech and expression. The restriction imposed later on in respect of the extent of this right, contains the word 'sedition'. An amendment has been moved here in regard to that. It is a matter of great pleasure that it seeks the deletion of the word 'sedition'. I would like to recall to the mind of honourable Members of the first occasion when section 124 A was included in the Indian Penal Code. I believe they remember that this section was specially framed for securing the conviction of Lokamanya Bal Gangadhar Tilak. Since then, many of us have been convicted under this section. In this connection many things that happened to me come to my mind. I belong to a family which was renowned in the Central Provinces for its loyalty. We had a tradition of being granted titles. My grandfather held the title of Raja and my uncle that of Diwan Bahadur and my father too that of Diwan Bahadur. I am very glad that titles will no more be granted in this country. In spite of belonging to such a family I was prosecuted under section 124A and that also for an interesting thing. My great grandfather had been awarded a gold waist-band inlaid with diamonds. The British Government awarded it to him for helping it in 1857 and the words 'In recognition of his services during the Mutiny in 1857' were engraved on it. In the course of my speech during the Satyagraha movement of 1930, I said that my great-grandfather got this waist-band for helping the alien government and that he had committed a sin by doing so and that I wanted to have engraved on it that the sin committed by my great-grandfather in helping to keep such a government in existence had been expiated by the great-grandson by seeking to uproot it. For this I was prosecuted under section 124 A and sentenced to two years' rigorous imprisonment. I mean to say that there must be many Members of this House who must have been sentenced under this article to undergo long periods of imprisonment. It is a matter of pleasure that we will now have freedom of speech and expression under this sub-clause and the word 'sedition' is also going to disappear.[23]

Consequently, the word 'sedition' was dropped from Article 13 of the draft Constitution. The freedom of speech and expression appeared in Article 19 (originally Article 13) in the final Constitution of India as Article 19(1)(a) with 19(2) placing certain restrictions on it.

However, the constitutionality of Section 124A of the IPC was in doubt after the removal of 'sedition' from Article 19 as well as because of Article 13, which provides that any law existing as on the date of the commencement of the Constitution, that is, 26 January 1950, would be void to the extent it was inconsistent with fundamental rights under Part III of the Constitution.

Sedition under Section 124A of the IPC continued to be a statutory offence as Article 372 of the Constitution provides that any existing law in force in India as on 26 January 1950 would continue to be in force unless explicitly modified or repealed by the legislature. Now that 'sedition' had been dropped as a restriction on the fundamental right to freedom of speech and expression, Section 124A of the IPC should ideally have been declared void by Parliament.

However, that never happened.

9

Courting Sedition: Conflict with Freedom of Speech

To recap, the Federal Court of India in the *Niharendu Dutt Majumdar*[1] case had held that incitement of public disorder, or the reasonable anticipation of that happening, was the gist of the offence of sedition under Section 124A of the IPC. Therefore, it was held that a speech or piece of writing must either actually incite disorder to be seditious, or reasonable people must be satisfied that such speech or piece of writing definitely intended to, or had the tendency to, incite disorder. This judgment was overturned by the Privy Council in the *Sadashiv Narayan Bhalerao*[2] case and the earlier position of law was restored.

Therefore, as India became a Constitutional Republic, any act which could excite disaffection, hatred or disloyalty against the government of India would be considered seditious under Section 124A of the IPC, irrespective of whether there was any incitement of disorder or not.

Section 124A[3] now read as:

Sedition.—Whoever, by words, either spoken or written, or by signs, or by visible representation, or otherwise, brings or attempts to bring into hatred or contempt, or excites or attempts to excite disaffection towards, the Government established by law in India, shall be punished with imprisonment for life,[4] to which fine may be added, or with imprisonment which may extend to three years, to which fine may be added, or with fine.

Explanation 1.—The expression 'disaffection' includes disloyalty and all feelings of enmity.

Explanation 2.—Comments expressing disapprobation of the measures of the Government with a view to obtain their alteration by lawful means, without exciting or attempting to excite hatred, contempt or disaffection, do not constitute an offence under this section.

Explanation 3.—Comments expressing disapprobation of the administrative or other action of the Government without exciting or attempting to excite hatred, contempt or disaffection, do not constitute an offence under this section.

No court can take cognizance of any offence under Section 124A of the IPC, or conspiracy to commit sedition, without prior sanction from the central government or the state government, as the case may be, as mandated by Section 196 of the Criminal Procedure Code, 1973. This provision existed even under the previous Criminal Procedure Code of 1898 and was in force till it was superseded by the 1973 Code. The object of requirement of prior sanction is to ensure prosecution only when after due consideration the appropriate sanctioning authority is satisfied that there is a proper case to put an accused on trial, and also to prevent wastage of judicial time as needless prosecutions would never result in convictions.

The first challenge to Section 124A of the IPC was launched in 1950 itself before the High Court of Punjab by one Tara Singh Gopi Chand[5] against whom two prosecutions under Section 124A and Section 153A[6] of the Code had been initiated in Karnal and Ludhiana districts in Punjab. The petitioner challenged the constitutional validity of the two provisions. Ironically, instead of accepting the strict interpretation of Section 124A as laid down in *Niharendu Dutt Majumdar,* the High Court accepted the position as settled by the Privy Council in *Sadashiv Narayan Bhalerao.* Therefore, it held that incitement of public disorder was not necessary for the invocation of Section 124A. Having found so, the High Court had no doubt that Section 124A was a restriction on freedom of speech granted under Article 19(1) (a) and tested it to see whether it was protected under Article 19(2) or not.

The Court found:

India is now a sovereign democratic State. Governments may go and be caused to go without the foundations of the State being impaired. A law of sedition thought necessary during a period of foreign rule has become inappropriate by the very nature of the change which has come about. It is true that the framers of the Constitution have not adopted the limitations which the Federal Court desired to lay down. It may be they did not consider it proper to go so far. The limitation placed by Clause (2) of Article 19 upon interference with the freedom of Speech, however, is real and substantial. The unsuccessful attempt to excite bad feelings is an offence within the ambit of Section

124A. In some instances at least the unsuccessful attempt will not undermine or tend to overthrow the State. It is enough if one instance appears of the possible application of the section to curtailment of the freedom of speech and expression in a manner not permitted by the constitution. The section then must be held to have become void.

It relied on two full-bench[7] judgments of the Supreme Court in *Romesh Thapar v. State of Madras*[8] and *Brij Bhushan v. State of Delhi*,[9] which had observed that Section 124A would be unconstitutional as the Constituent Assembly had deleted 'sedition' from Article 13 (which was enacted as Article 19) and therefore the provision would be in violation of the fundamental right to speech and expression. However, the two judgments did not explicitly declare Section 124A as unconstitutional as it was adjudicating on the constitutionality of other statutory provisions. Justice Sayid Fazl Ali dissented in both cases and observed that Section 124A would not be unconstitutional. To reach such a conclusion he relied on the 'incitement of public disorder' interpretation in *Niharendu Dutt Majumdar* and thus felt that the law against sedition would be an exempted restriction under Article 19(2).

The Punjab High Court, therefore, concluded that Section 124A of the IPC had become void as it contravened the freedom of speech and expression guaranteed by Article 19 of the Constitution. As a bonus offering, it also held Section 153A to be unconstitutional.

Parliament did not view these judgments, among others, favourably and deemed it necessary to amend Article 19 to negate the effect of these judgments by way of the Constitution (First Amendment) Act, 1951. According to the statement of objects and reasons of the amending

Act, citizens' right to freedom of speech and expression guaranteed by Article 19(1)(a) had been held by some courts to be so comprehensive as not to render a person culpable even if he advocates murder and other crimes of violence. It argued that this was unlike other countries with written constitutions where freedom of speech and press was not regarded as debarring the State from punishing or preventing the abuse of such freedom.

The amending Act modified Article 19(2) to protect the State's power to provide 'reasonable' restrictions on freedom of speech by extending the power to do so in the interest of public order, security of State, friendly relations with foreign States and to prevent incitement of an offence. These restrictions were in addition to the exemptions provided under the original Article 19(2). The freshly amended Article 19 was made effective retrospectively, as if it had been in the Constitution since it came into force.

During the debate on the amending Act, Prime Minister Jawaharlal Nehru referred to the offence of sedition under Section 124A of the IPC and called it highly objectionable and obnoxious. He felt it should not have a place in Indian law for both practical and historical reasons and it would be better to get rid of the provision at the earliest.[10]

He would know, having gone to prison for being seditious by his own admission. Despite making the right noises, even Nehru's government never made an attempt to repeal Section 124A.

The first constitutional challenge to Section 124A after the first constitutional amendment occurred before the Patna High Court in the case of *Debi Soren & Ors v. State of Bihar*.[11]

There was an annual conference of the *Bhagalpur Adivasi Mahasabha* held in Santal Parganas district in Bihar over three days in March 1949. One Debi Soren presided over the conference. He and the other two accused, Hanna Bodra and Yunus Soren, were the principal speakers. The prosecution alleged that on two days the accused made seditious speeches at the conference against the government of Bihar. The accused had made speeches claiming that the government was repressing the tribal population in the state and called for the ouster of non-tribal Biharis from their lands. The three accused were convicted of sedition by the magistrate against which they filed an appeal before the Patna High Court.

The appellants relied upon the judgment of the Punjab High Court in the *Tara Chand* case to content that Section 124A of the IPC had become void as it contravened the freedom of speech guaranteed under Article 19(1) of the Constitution. The appellants also relied on the judgments of the Supreme Court in *Brij Bhushan* and *Romesh Thapar,* which were based on the interpretation of Section 124A by the Privy Council in the *Sadashiv Narayan* case.

However, the High Court held that the judgments were no longer good law because of the amendment of Article 19(2) to include 'public order'. It stated, 'If the Section is read as a whole together with the explanations, it seems clear that the mischief which it contemplates has a reference to public order in its widest sense, even though the section does not make it necessary that there should be a direct incitement to violence or disorder. My view is that even accepting the interpretation put upon the section by their Lordships of the Privy Council, the restrictions it imposes on freedom of speech and expression are reasonable restrictions in the interests of public order . . . From this point of view, Clause (2) of Article 19, as it now stands, saves the provisions of Sections 124A and 153A, Penal Code.'

While the Patna High Court upheld the constitutional validity of Section 124A, another post-amendment constitutional challenge to Section 124A arose in the north-eastern state of Manipur.[12]

A public meeting was organized at the polo ground in Imphal on 19 April 1953 where the accused published and circulated leaflets against the Indian State. The accused threatened satyagraha for their demand for the creating of an independent 'buffer state' of Manipur under the trusteeship of the United Nations. A prosecution under Sections 124A and 153A of the IPC was launched against the accused who were convicted under both provisions by the magistrate.

On an appeal being filed before the High Court of Manipur, it was contended that Sections 124A and 153A had become void on account of being inconsistent with Articles 19(1)(a) and 19(2) of the Constitution. The High Court took note of the judgments in *Brij Bhushan, Romesh Thapar* and *Tara Singh* to observe that Section 124A had been declared unconstitutional but the first amendment to the Constitution necessitated a re-look at the question.

The High Court noted that the amended Article 19(2) enabled the State to make laws imposing reasonable restrictions on freedom of speech in the interest of security of the State, to maintain public order and to prevent incitement of an offence. It relied on the 'public order' test laid down in the *Niharendu Dutt Majumdar* case and accepted that mere criticism of the government without inciting an offence would not be punishable in the interest of 'public order'. In doing so it went with the minority dissent in *Brij Bhushan* and *Romesh Thapar* judgments provided by Justice Fazl Ali.

Therefore, the Manipur High Court held that Section 124A of the IPC was partially unconstitutional to the extent it sought to impose restrictions on freedom of speech insofar as a speech merely excites or tends to excite disaffection against the government. However, if such an action results in the incitement of violence or public disorder then punishment for sedition would not be unconstitutional.

What the Patna High Court in *Debi Soren* saved completely, the Manipur High Court destroyed partially.

For good measure, in 1958 the Allahabad High Court also entered the fray in the interpretation of Section 124A vis-a-vis Article 19 of the Constitution.

One Ram Nandan was convicted of sedition by a sessions judge for delivering a speech to about 200 villagers. He attacked the Congress government which, he alleged, was responsible for poverty, food scarcity, inflation and high taxation. He claimed that the labourers of Uttar Pradesh had now organized themselves and would overthrow the government through armed revolt if it did not concede to their demands. As a parting shot, he termed Jawaharlal Nehru a traitor, blaming him for the partition of India.

In an appeal against his conviction, Ram Nandan challenged the constitutional validity of Section 124A of the IPC. The High Court relied on the line of judgments in *Brij Bhushan, Romesh Thapar* and *Debi Soren* and held that danger to public order is not an ingredient of the offence of sedition. Consequently, it held that the restriction imposed on the right to freedom of speech by Section 124A cannot be said to be in the interests of public order. It was of the view that a restriction imposed on certain speeches would be in the interests of public order but not that imposed on other speeches which do not contain a threat to public order. Therefore, it did not find anything in Section 124A to distinguish between the two classes of speeches and thus did not deem it to be a reasonable restriction under Article 19(2) of the Constitution. The High Court disagreed with the Patna High Court's judgment in *Debi Soren,* despite relying on it for interpretation of the provision, and held Section 124A to be unconstitutional for being in contravention of Article 19(1) of the Constitution.[13]

In summation, the Patna High Court found Section 124A to be constitutional; the Manipur High Court found it to be partly unconstitutional; and the Allahabad High Court found it to be unconstitutional. Thus, at this stage the score stood 1.5 to 1 against Section 124A of the IPC.

This difference of opinion between the three High Courts could now only be settled by the Supreme Court of India, and it did so in the landmark judgment in *Kedar Nath Singh v. State of Bihar*.[14]

Singh, who was a member of the Forward Communist Party, was prosecuted for sedition for delivering a speech in the Munger district of Bihar on 26 May 1953. He was alleged to have said, 'Today the dogs of the C.I.D. are loitering round Barauni. Many official dogs are sitting even in this meeting. The people of India drove out the Britishers from this country and elected these Congress goondas to the gaddi and seated them on it. Today these Congress goondas are sitting on the gaddi due to mistake of the people. When we drove out the Britishers, we shall strike and turn out these Congress goondas as well. These official dogs will also be liquidated along with these Congress goondas . . . The Forward Communist Party does not believe in the doctrine of vote itself. The party had always been believing in revolution and does so even at present. We believe in that revolution, which will come and in the flames of which the capitalists, zamindars and the Congress leaders of India, who have made it their profession to loot the country, will be reduced to ashes and on their ashes will be established a Government of the poor and the downtrodden people of India.'

His speech was found to be seditious by the trial court which sentenced him to one year's rigorous imprisonment. His appeal against conviction was also dismissed by the Patna High Court, after which he filed an appeal before the

Supreme Court. The appeal was decided by a constitution bench comprising five judges led by Chief Justice Bhuvneshwar Sinha.

The appeal was heard together with other appeals which had the common question of law regarding the constitutionality of Section 124A of the IPC. The first connected case was of Mohammad Ishaq Ilmi who was prosecuted for having delivered a speech at Aligarh as chairman of the Reception Committee of the All India Muslim Convention on 30 October 1953. His speech on that occasion was prosecuted for being seditious and he was convicted under Section 124A. In the second connected case, one Rama had been convicted of sedition for advocating the use of violence to overthrow the government in a speech delivered on 29 May 1954 at a meeting of the Bolshevik Party in an Uttar Pradesh village.

In the third case, one Parasnath Tripathi was accused of sedition for delivering a speech in the district of Faizabad on 26 September 1955 in which he is said to have exhorted the audience to organize a volunteer army and resist the government and its servants by violent means. When he was arrested for trial, he filed a writ petition challenging his arrest as illegal on the basis that Section 124A was void as being in contravention of his fundamental rights of free speech and expression. This petition was clubbed with appeals filed by Mohammad Ishaq Ilmi and Rama before the Allahabad High Court which took the view that Section 124A of the IPC was unconstitutional. The High Court therefore acquitted Ilmi and Rama and quashed proceedings against Tripathi. The state government duly challenged the judgment before the Supreme Court.

The Supreme Court first carried out the exercise of interpreting Section 124A to establish its actual meaning and application. It went through the history of the provision and compared the judgments in *Niharendu Dutt Majumdar* and *Sadashiv Narayan*. It reached the conclusion that any written or spoken words which have implicit in them the idea of subverting the government by violent means, akin to the term 'revolution', have been made penal by Section 124A of the IPC. However, it found that the explanations to the section clarify that strong words used to express disapprobation of the measures of the government with a view to reform by lawful means would not be seditious. It also observed that criticism of the government, however harsh, which did not incite public disorder through violence, would not be seditious either.

Having held so, it felt that it was duty bound to clearly demarcate between the scope of a citizen's fundamental right to free speech and the power of lawmakers to impose reasonable restrictions in the interest of security of the State and public order. Towards this end, the court fell back upon the Federal Court's interpretation in *Niharendu Dutt Majumdar* that the gist of the offence of sedition is incitement to violence or the tendency or the intention to create public disorders by words spoken or written. It felt that interpreting Section 124A on these lines would protect it from being void, as compared to the interpretation given by the Privy Council which held that incitement of violence or public disorder was irrelevant. Therefore, the constitution bench of the Supreme Court read the 'public order' test into Section 124A to protect it from the scourge of unconstitutionality. It held that Section 124A would be within the permissible limits of reasonable restriction laid down in Article 19(2) of the Constitution.

This judgment has settled the question of the constitutionality of the sedition law, for now. As it is a judgment of a constitution bench of the Supreme Court, which comprises of five judges, it can only be overruled by a bench comprising of seven judges or higher. Since *Kedar Nath Singh* the issue has not been diverged from by any High Court or the Supreme Court as the decision is binding on all courts across the country. As per Supreme Court Rules it would take a reference to a seven-judge bench by any other bench of the Supreme Court in an appropriate case to reopen the question.

One question which arises is whether this judgment can be looked at with a strict legal perspective or do we need to look at the political context as well. The judgment was delivered in January of 1962. The year is important because that was the year of the Sino-India conflict at the northern border in Jammu and Kashmir, and in the North-East Frontier Agency (NEFA), which is present-day Arunachal Pradesh. Trouble had been brewing on India's border with Tibet and China for some years, which escalated in 1959 after India had provided sanctuary to the Dalai Lama after his escape from Tibet. The tension and constant squabbles between the Indian armed forces and the People's Liberation Army of China culminated in the war of 1962.[15]

Now, Kedar Nath was a member of a communist organization and admittedly making anti-government speeches with calls for a labour revolution at a time when the Communist Party of India was considered the fifth pillar of the Chinese invasion due to its pro-China stance.[16] Such unravelling events could have had a bearing on the minds of the judges, who were only human. The Communist Party of India had even emerged as one of the largest opposition parties after the 1957 general elections.[17] In such circumstances, in the face of a major border dispute with China which was compounded by a rise in communist thought within India, arguably the continued presence of Section 124A of the IPC may have been deemed necessary.

One can only speculate.

One's speculation does find support in the decision of the Madhya Pradesh High Court in *State of Madhya Pradesh v. Baleshwar Dayal & Ors*[18] decided in May 1966. In the instant case the accused were charged with offences under the Defence of India Rules, 1962 which was a war-time emergency measure not unlike the British-era measures. The prosecution was launched under Rule 41(5) of the Rules for publication of articles in early 1963. These articles were critical of the Indian government and the cadre of Indian army officers.

Rule 41(5) was similar to Section 124A, as acknowledged by the High Court, and the accused were charged with 'prejudicial acts likely to cause disaffection among that armed forces, prejudice and interference with the recruitment and the discipline among such forces, bringing them into hatred and contempt and the exciting of disaffection towards the government in general, and of the officers in particular and finally to prejudice the conduct of the military operations'. The accused were acquitted by the trial court for lack of evidence of any direct adverse effect being caused due to the articles. However, the High Court reversed the acquittal and convicted the accused based on the Privy Council interpretation and thus did away with the 'public order' test.

It did so because it distinguished the emergency measure under the Defence of India Rules from the more general Section 124A. In convicting the accused the High Court observed, 'Coming to the punishment we note that the incidents that have led to these communications are fast becoming matters of history. Besides, there have been many nearer events which have, as it were, blacked out of public memory a good deal of the happenings of 1962. But we have to make it clear that there are prejudicial acts, highly prejudicial in fact, and subversive of the strength and morale of the armed forces.'

Clearly, geopolitical events and the Indo-China war had an effect on the adjudication in this case to such an extent that the High Court deviated from the interpretation of sedition provided by the Supreme Court in *Kedar Nath*.

In fact, Jawaharlal Nehru had established a National Integration Council in 1961 which held its first meeting on 2 June 1962. The Committee on National Integration and Regionalism appointed by the National Integration Council recommended that Article 19 of the Constitution be so amended that adequate powers become available for the preservation and maintenance of the integrity and sovereignty of the Union. With that in mind, Parliament amended clause (2), along with (3) and (4), of Article 19 to enable the State to make any law imposing reasonable restrictions on the exercise of the rights conferred by Article 19(1) in the interests of the sovereignty and integrity of India. Therefore, the government was further empowered to make laws reasonably curbing free speech to protect the sovereignty and integrity of India.[19]

The conflict with China made the Indian State even more wary of communists, especially Maoists. In 1971, the government of Gujarat passed an order of forfeiture of all copies of a book in the Gujarati language which contained passages from speeches delivered by Mao Zedong, the father of the communist movement and ideology in China. Such forfeiture was ordered on the ground that the book contained seditious material, the publication of which would be punishable under Section 124A of the IPC. According to the government, the book was full of hatred and contempt for persons who did not subscribe to the communist ideology, and contained advice on how to overthrow a non-communist government and establish a communist government through violent revolution.

The government had exercised this power under Section 99A of the erstwhile Criminal Procedure Code, 1898, which empowered the State to order the forfeiture of copies of books, newspapers, etc., for being seditious. This code was soon repealed and substituted by a new code in 1973.

The order was challenged before the Gujarat High Court by the publisher Manubhai Patel. The court applied the *Kedar Nath* interpretation strictly and held[20] that the book dealt with a wide variety of topics which reflected the principles and practice of communism as enunciated by Mao. The purpose of the book was to acquaint readers with his world view and ideology and not to incite violence or create public disorder. The court could not find even a word in the book which suggested that people should overthrow lawfully established government in India by force or violence.

Therefore, according to the court, to condemn the book as seditious would be to close the doors of knowledge to ostracize a philosophy because it challenged values held by the Indian society. It observed that:

It is not for the Government of the day nor for the Judges presiding over our Courts to decide what doctrine of philosophy is good for our people. It is for the people to choose what is best for them and in order that they may be able to make a wise and intelligent choice, free propagation of ideas is an essential requisite. The ideas propagated may be unorthodox and unconventional: they may disturb the complacency of a handful minority or they may challenge deep seated, sacred beliefs and question the most fundamental postulates of our social, political or economic thinking. That should be no ground for anxiety or apprehension, particularly in

a country like ours which has always believed in the
pursuit of truth and in its unending search for truth,
never hesitated to receive new ideas and absorb
them, if found acceptable. There can indeed be no
real freedom unless thought is free and unchecked,
not free thought for those who agree with us but
freedom for the thought we hate. It is only from
clash of ideas that truth can emerge, for the best
test of truth is the power of the thought to get itself
accepted in the competition of the market.

Thus, the High Court held that the passages in the book
were not of a kind which would attract the exercise of
power of forfeiture as it did not constitute seditious matter
punishable under Section 124A of the IPC.

The communist threat, however, resulted in a finding
of sedition in the case of *P. Hemlatha v. State of Andhra
Pradesh*[21] decided by the High Court of Andhra Pradesh
in April 1976. Despite staying with the interpretation of
sedition as enunciated in the *Kedar Nath* judgment, the
High Court gave a finding of sedition against a publication
of poems despite the absence of any evidence of public order
or tranquillity being disturbed. It is pertinent to note that
in 1976 India was going through a period of peacetime
emergency declared by the Indira Gandhi government on
the ground of 'internal disturbance'.

In one poem '. . . the utterances have a tendency to
create disorder or disturbance of public peace by resort
to violence', according to the Court. In another offending
poem the principles professed and practised by communist
insurgents were commended and people were exhorted to
sharpen their weapons '. . . to cut down the pests and the
leeches on the lines taught by naxalite leaders' who did
not believe in the existence and functioning of government

established by law. The last poem declared, 'We do not rest till we overthrow with arms, the Government which does not come down with the strike.'

The High Court found that the writings incited and advocated the overthrow of the government by violent and unlawful means, thus endangering public peace and security of the State. 'They have the pernicious tendency or intention of creating public disorder or disturbance of public tranquillity and "law and order". The very security of the State depends upon the maintenance of law and order', it found upon employing the 'sovereignty and integrity' test along with the 'public order' test.

It further held that the writings in question were not protected by the explanations to Section 124A and also held that even truth was not a justification for seditious utterances. In doing so, the High Court regressed to a colonial common law interpretation of sedition where this argument had been utilized to subdue nationalist movements.

Years later, the Supreme Court underlined the interpretation of Section 124A on the basis of the 'public order' test laid down in *Kedar Nath*.

Balwant Singh and Bhupinder Singh, two Punjab government employees, were arrested on 31 October 1984 at about 5:45 p.m. in Chandigarh. Earlier that day, at about 9 a.m., approximately 250 kilometres away in Delhi, Prime Minister Indira Gandhi was shot by her Sikh bodyguards Beant Singh and Satwant Singh as retribution for Operation Blue Star.[22] She was declared dead at the All India Institute of Medical Sciences (AIIMS) at 2:23 p.m.[23]

Balwant Singh and Bhupinder Singh were charged with sedition, among other charges, for raising slogans saying 'Khalistan Zindabad' (Long live Khalistan), 'Raj karega Khalsa' (Sikhs will rule forever) and 'Hinduan nun Punjab chon kadh ke chhadange, hun mauka aya hai raj kayam

karan da' (This is an opportunity to establish our rule, will
ensure that Hindus leave Punjab). They were convicted
for sedition under Section 124A, as well as for promoting
enmity and hatred under Section 153A, by a Special TADA
Court in March 1985.

On an appeal filed before the Supreme Court, it held
that as the slogans were raised only a couple of times only
by the accused and that they did not evoke any response
from any other person of the Sikh community or any other
community, it was difficult to hold that 'upon the raising of
such casual slogans, a couple of times without any other act
whatsoever the charge of sedition can be founded. It is not
the prosecution case that the appellants were either leading
a procession or were otherwise raising the slogans with
the intention to incite people to create disorder or that the
slogans in fact created any law and order problem . . . the
people, in general, were un-affected and carried on with their
normal activities. The casual raising of the Slogans, once or
twice by two individuals alone cannot be said to be aimed at
exciting or attempt to excite hatred or disaffection towards
the Government as established by law in India, Section
124A IPC, would in the facts and circumstances of the case
have no application whatsoever and would not be attracted
to the facts and circumstances of the case.'[24]

The Supreme Court further observed that raising some
slogans only a couple of times by two lone persons, which
neither evoked any response nor any reaction from any
member of the public, can neither attract the provisions
of Section 124A or Section 153A of the IPC. It held that
'Some more overt act was required to bring home the
charge to the two appellants, who are Government servants.
The police officials exhibited lack of maturity and more
of sensitivity in arresting the appellants for raising the
slogans . . . keeping in view the tense situation prevailing

on the date of the assassination of Smt. Indira Gandhi . . . Raising of some lonesome slogans, a couple of times by two individuals, without anything more, did not constitute any threat to the Government of India as by law established nor could the same give rise to feelings of enmity or hatred among different communities or religious or other groups.'

Though it did not explicitly rely on *Kedar Nath*, the Supreme Court emphasized on the test that speech alleged to be seditious must have a direct bearing on the disturbance of public order. Isolated acts of sloganeering or provocative speeches would not fulfil the requirements under Section 124A.

Two years later, the Supreme Court again explicitly re-emphasized the principles of the *Kedar Nath* and *Balwant Singh* judgments in the case of *Bilal Ahmad Kaloo v. State of Andhra Pradesh*[25] and acquitted the accused who had been convicted for sedition as well as for promoting enmity and hatred under Section 153A of the IPC.

Bilal Ahmad Kaloo was allegedly an active member of a militant outfit called Al-Jehad which was formed with the ultimate object of liberating Kashmir from the Indian Union. He was accused of spreading communal hatred among Muslim youth in Hyderabad and for encouraging them to undergo training in armed militancy. On his arrest he was found to be in possession of a countrymade revolver and live cartridges. He was also accused of propagating among Muslims that Muslims in Kashmir were being subjected to atrocities by the Indian army. He was arrested after a series of bomb blasts occurred in Hyderabad in 1993.

The Supreme Court relied on *Kedar Nath* and found that the decisive ingredient for establishing the offence of sedition under Section 124A is the doing of certain acts which would bring the government established by law in India into hatred or contempt. In Bilal Ahmad Kaloo's case, there was not even a suggestion by the prosecution that he did anything against the government of India or any other state government. It found that, 'As the charge framed against the appellant is totally bereft of the crucial allegation that appellant did anything with reference to the Government it is not possible to sustain the conviction of the appellant under Section 124A IPC.'

While acquitting Kaloo, the Supreme Court took a parting shot at the state of the criminal justice system when dealing with offences like sedition and heavily criticized the mechanical approach taken by the trial court. It admonished them by saying:

> Before parting with this judgment, we wish to observe that the manner in which convictions have been recorded for offences under Section 153A, 124A and 505(2), has exhibited a very casual approach of the trial court. Let alone the absence of any evidence which may attract the provisions of the sections, as already observed, even the charges framed against the appellant for these offences did not contain the essential ingredients of the offences under the three sections. The appellant strictly speaking should not have been put to trial for those offences. Mechanical order convicting a citizen for offences of such serious nature like sedition and to promote enmity and hatred etc. does harm to the cause. It is expected that graver the offence, greater should be the care taken so that the liberty of a citizen is not lightly interfered with.

One would think subordinate courts would take the observations and findings of the Supreme Court in *Balwant Singh* and *Bilal Ahmad Kaloo* to heart in adjudicating on cases where the offence of sedition is alleged. However, subsequent cases have demonstrated that Indian courts still have a long way to go to protect the freedom of speech and liberty guaranteed to citizens.

The case of Dr Binayak Sen demonstrates how the trial court and High Court failed to apply the principles laid down by the Supreme Court. Dr Sen was accused of sedition for meeting Narayan Sanyal, an alleged Maosit insurgent, thirty-three times in 2006 and 2007 while Sanyal was lodged in Raipur jail in Chhattisgarh. He was also alleged to be a conduit for Sanyal to disseminate his letters. During the course of searching Dr Sen's house, the police discovered a booklet of the Communist Party of India (ML), a letter written by a Maoist lodged in jail to Dr Sen, printed material on 'Andhra Pradesh: Women's Rights and Naxalite Groups', paper cuttings relating to human rights and atrocities of the police, and a booklet on Salwa Judum. Dr Sen is in fact a medical doctor and was a member of the People's Union for Civil Liberties, and also general secretary of the Chhattisgarh Lok Swatantrya Sangathan.[26]

Based on the allegations and the material discovered in his possession, the trial court convicted him of sedition in December 2010 and sentenced him to rigorous imprisonment for life. Dr Sen challenged the verdict before the High Court of Chhattisgarh which refused to grant him bail, less on the merit of his case but more on an ideological basis.[27]

The Supreme Court on the other hand granted him bail and suspended his sentence in April 2011, while not passing a detailed order so as to not prejudice the appeal pending before the High Court.[28] While deciding his petition, the court observed that no case of sedition appeared to have been made out against Dr Sen. It reportedly asked how sedition could be established merely on the basis of Dr

Sen meeting Sanyal thirty-three times and his possession of Maoist literature.[29]

Dr Sen's appeal against his conviction is still pending before the Chhattisgarh High Court.

10

Stories of Sedition

Asia Cup 2014. India vs Pakistan on 2 March at the Sher-e-Bangla Stadium in Mirpur, Bangladesh. A thriller of a match.

No other cricketer in his generation blends genius so liberally with lunacy as Shahid Afridi, and though there were glimpses of both in Mirpur, Afridi sent Pakistan's fans into raptures and endeared himself to them again, as only he can, with two mighty blows during an incredibly tense final over. The India–Pakistan clash was given a finish deserving of its profile, as Pakistan ran India's 245 down with two balls and one wicket remaining.[1]

Pakistan won a virtual semi-final with one wicket remaining in the last over of the match. The result would surely have caused many television sets to be smashed across India. It also resulted in sixty-seven Kashmiri students being arrested for sedition in Meerut, Uttar Pradesh.

Indians take their cricket very seriously. So seriously that some of them felt that Kashmiri students cheering for

Pakistan and celebrating its win over India would cause incitement of public disorder and violence against the State!

The *New York Times* summed up the situation perfectly, 'Cricket is a national obsession in India. Some Kashmiris root against the Indian team because of resentment from decades of national policies there, including routine arrests of pro-independence figures and thousands of disappearances.'[2] These young men were students of the Swami Vivekanand Subharati University in Meerut. The vice chancellor of the university lodged a complaint against these students, following which the Uttar Pradesh Police arrested them for sedition under Section 124A and—its old friend and companion—incitement of hatred between communities under Section 153A of the IPC. The arrests made national headlines and provoked Omar Abdullah, then chief minister of Jammu and Kashmir, to call for quashing the charges. Even the Indian Home Ministry called for a report on the arrests. In the face of this unwanted limelight, four days later the state government dropped the sedition charges against the students. However, the other charges remained, and the students were thrown out of their university-provided accommodation.[3]

If you found this to be indiscriminate and vexatious, wait till I tell you about a cartoonist who got arrested for sedition.

Aseem Trivedi was arrested in September 2012 after a First Information Report (FIR) under Section 124A of the IPC was lodged against him for spreading hatred and disrespect against the government through his cartoons published on a website called 'India against Corruption'. The offending cartoons had also been displayed at the MMRDA ground in Mumbai as a nationwide anti-corruption campaign launched by Anna Hazare, a social activist. Trivedi's cartoons were alleged to have defamed Parliament, the

Constitution of India and the national emblem. He was granted bail and released from Arthur Road Jail, Mumbai, after an individual filed a public interest litigation before the Bombay High Court.[4]

Subsequently, based on an opinion of the advocate general of Maharashtra, sedition charges under Section 124A against Trivedi were dropped. The High Court, however, did not let the matter go. First of all, it made clear that it really did not like the cartoons as they lacked 'wit or humour' and were full of 'anger and disgust against corruption prevailing in the political system'. However, it emphasized that the State could not have encroached upon Trivedi's freedom to express indignation against corruption in the political system in strong terms or visual representations, especially when there was absolutely no allegation of incitement to violence, or the tendency or the intention to create public disorder.

The High Court thereafter directed the state government to issue guidelines to all police personnel in Maharashtra to be followed in cases of sedition under Section 124A, such as:

(i) The words, signs or representations must bring the Government (Central or State) into hatred or contempt or must cause or attempt to cause disaffection, enmity or disloyalty to the Government and the words/signs/ representation must also be an incitement to violence or must be intended or tend to create public disorder or a reasonable apprehension of public disorder;

(ii) Words, signs or representations against politicians or public servants by themselves do not fall in this category unless the words/signs/ representations show them as representative of the Government;

(iii) Comments expressing disapproval or criticism of the Government with a view to obtaining a change of government by lawful means without any of the above are not seditious under Section 124A;

(iv) Obscenity or vulgarity by itself should not be taken into account as a factor or consideration for deciding whether a case falls within the purview of Section 124A of IPC, for they are covered under other sections of law;

(v) A legal opinion in writing which gives reasons addressing the aforesaid must be obtained from Law Officer of the District followed within two weeks by a legal opinion in writing from Public Prosecutor of the State.[5]

The High Court basically read back the provision for the benefit of the state police and also imposed a requirement of obtaining reasons and legal opinion prior to the initiation of a prosecution for sedition. The judgment, though, applies to the police in the state of Maharashtra only, and is not canon for any other state police.

Now, while the law says that before any court can take cognizance of any offence under Section 124A of the IPC, there should be prior sanction to prosecute under Section 196 of the Criminal Procedure Code. In simple words, charges cannot be framed against persons accused of sedition unless the government approves and sanctions the charge sheet filed by the prosecution. So, under law, there is only a requirement to obtain sanction for trial, but no requirement to obtain sanction before arrest for sedition.

The Bombay High Court in Trivedi's case made an attempt to impose some mechanism for arrest for sedition in Maharashtra. However, nationally, there is absolutely no uniformity in tackling cases of sedition.

Common Cause, an NGO, along with S.P. Udayakumar brought the situation to the notice of the Supreme Court by way of a public interest writ petition[6] in 2016. Udayakumar was in fact an aggrieved petitioner who was facing several sedition cases for protesting against the Kudankulam nuclear power plant in Tamil Nadu. More on that later.

The petition drew attention to the 1979 ratification of the International Covenant on Civil and Political Rights, which sets forth standards for safeguarding freedom of speech internationally. Considering the misuse of Section 124A beyond the scope set down in *Kedar Nath,* and in light of convention obligations, the petition sought to protect bona fide activists from misuse of sedition law to suppress civil rights campaigns. The loophole regarding no requirement of sanction prior to arrest was being exploited by the police and administration to muzzle dissenting voices. The punishment lay in the procedure for such accused persons.

Common Cause and Udayakumar therefore prayed for directions from the Supreme Court making it mandatory to obtain a reasoned order from the concerned director general of police in the state or the commissioner of police, as the case may be, certifying that any alleged seditious act either led to violence or had the tendency to incite violence before an FIR being registered or the accused being arrested. Incidentally, the petition was argued by Prashant Bhushan, a leading public interest advocate who had been assaulted in the past for comments on the political situation in Kashmir, and who had a complaint registered against him by an individual claiming that his comments advocating a referendum in Kashmir were seditious.

The Supreme Court, however, missed an opportunity to emulate the Bombay High Court. While deciding the petition on 9 September 2016, it simply passed an order that authorities while dealing with cases under Section 124A shall be guided by the principles laid down in *Kedar Nath*. It refused to deal with the wider issues raised in the petition. The flaw with the order is that while *Kedar Nath* is definitely law of the land, it does not provide for pre-arrest requirements and compliances. Any person arrested for sedition will have to obtain bail, attend proceedings, make themselves present for investigations, etc., before the charge sheet is filed or the case is closed.

Take the example of the Jawaharlal Nehru University (JNU) sedition case.

On 9 February 2016, a poetry reading event called 'The country without a post office' was organized within the JNU campus in Delhi by the JNU Students Union (JNUSU). The poster of the event had 'The country without a post office. The struggle of people against power is struggle of memory against forgetting' printed on the front, and 'Against the Brahmanical collective conscience against the judicial killing of Afzal Guru & Maqbool Bhat, in solidarity with the struggle of Kashmiri people for their democratic right to self-determination, we invite you for a cultural evening of protests with poets, artists, singers, writers, students, intellectuals, cultural activists. 9th February, Thursday 5 PM, Sabarmati Dhaba. There will also be an art exhibition and a photo exhibition portraying the history of the occupation of Kashmir and in solidarity with the valiant people of Kashmir. Anirban, Anjali, Anwesha, Aswathi, Bhavna, Komal, Rayaz, Rubina, Umar, Sama' printed on the back.[7]

This poster was forwarded by the joint secretary of JNUSU, who was a member of the right-wing Akhil Bharatiya Vidyarthi Parishad (ABVP), to the security officer of JNU who in turn informed the police half an hour before the event could take place on 9 February.

The complaint anticipated 'anti-national' activities and 'anti-constitutional' slogans. When a police party reached JNU, it encountered a group of students led by Kanhaiya Kumar, the president of JNUSU, who was a member of the left-wing All India Students Federation (AISF), and Umar Khalid. Another group of students led by Saurabh Sharma, the aforementioned joint secretary of JNUSU, were moving towards the first group with the intention to oppose them. Both groups were kept separated from each other by the police and campus security till the time they dispersed at 8:30 p.m. after constant slogan-shouting at each other.

The next day, Zee News, a leading national news television channel, broadcast purported video footage of the protests with some students allegedly shouting anti-India and pro-Pakistan slogans. The FIR records that a faction of students led by Umar Khalid were allegedly shouting slogans like 'We won't tolerate Afzal's execution . . . We are with the Kashmiri youth who are struggling for freedom . . . abolish death penalty . . . freedom is our right . . . we will fight for our freedom . . . Pakistan zindabad'. The FIR alleging sedition was registered under Section 124A of the IPC based on this video.

Kanhaiya Kumar, Umar Khalid and Anirban Bhattacharya were arrested soon thereafter on the charge of sedition. Kanhaiya Kumar was brutally assaulted by lawyers at Patiala House Court[8] when he was being produced before a magistrate by the police.[9]

Justice Pratibha Rani of the Delhi High Court granted him interim bail on 2 March 2016 but not before pontificating on curing anti-nationalism. The judgment said:

> The reason behind anti-national views in the mind of students who raised slogans on the death anniversary of Afzal Guru, who was convicted for attack on our Parliament, which led to this situation

have not only to be found by them but remedial steps are also required to be taken in this regard by those managing the affairs of the JNU so that there is no recurrence of such incident. The investigation in this case is at nascent stage. The thoughts reflected in the slogans raised by some of the students of JNU who organized and participated in that programme cannot be claimed to be protected as fundamental right to freedom of speech and expression. I consider this as a kind of infection from which such students are suffering which needs to be controlled/cured before it becomes an epidemic. Whenever some infection is spread in a limb, effort is made to cure the same by giving antibiotics orally and if that does not work, by following second line of treatment. Sometimes it may require surgical intervention also. However, if the infection results in infecting the limb to the extent that it becomes gangrene, amputation is the only treatment. During the period spent by the petitioner in judicial custody, he might have introspected about the events that had taken place. To enable him to remain in the main stream, at present I am inclined to provide conservative method of treatment.[10]

The court released the petitioner on interim bail for a period of six months upon the condition that he would not participate in any activity which may be termed 'anti-national'. Such a condition was imposed even though nowhere in the law of the land is the term 'anti-national' or anti-nationalism defined. The bail order, though a positive outcome for Kanhaiya Kumar, went beyond what the court was called upon to adjudicate on and, dare I say, indulged in attacking a straw man.

For example, it observed that people were enjoying freedom of expression only because the nation's borders are guarded by Indian armed and paramilitary forces, especially in harsh terrain like the Siachen Glacier or the Rann of Kutch. It concluded that such slogans have an effect of threatening national integrity and may have demoralizing effects on the family of those slain soldiers 'who returned home in coffin draped in tricolor'.[11] If that is accepted to be logical, then even any legitimate criticism of the government or the armed forces would have the same effect.

Though the Court eventually clarified that its observations would not have any bearing on the merits of the case during trial, it is very difficult to ignore what it observed, especially for a trial court which is subordinate to the High Court in its jurisdiction.

As the High Court granted interim bail only for six months, which would have expired in September 2016, the three accused moved the magistrate's court for regular bail which was granted to them on 26 August. No charge sheet was, however, filed by the police for the next two-and-a-half years till 14 January 2019.[12] However, there was a twist in the tale as the magistrate on 19 January refused to accept the charge sheet which had been filed without prior approval from the state government.[13] At the time of writing this, the charge sheet had not been approved by the government.

We can only imagine what Justice Pratibha Rani would have said about the twenty-five-year-old M. Salman from Kerala who was booked for sedition for not standing up for the national anthem. He even posted derogatory comments against the national flag on his Facebook page. He was arrested in August 2014 and denied bail by the magistrate in Thiruvananthapuram. He filed a bail application before the Kerala High Court which granted him bail without expressing its views on whether his actions amounted to sedition or not.

However, the High Court imposed onerous conditions on Salman by demanding two sureties to furnish bail for him for Rs 1 lakh each. He was also directed to appear before the investigating officer on all Mondays and Fridays between 10:00 a.m. and 11:00 a.m. until the filing of the charge sheet. As the icing on the cake, he was made to surrender his passport and thus barred from travelling abroad.[14]

Despite going through this ordeal, Salman, who identifies himself as an anarchist, said, 'I never stand up when the National Anthem is sung and have no plans to do it in future too, because I think we should do what we believe in.'[15] You may not like what he did, or his world view, but it is settled law that such an act cannot be considered sedition. There was no incitement of, or tendency to cause, violence, just like in the case of *Balwant Singh*. Despite such a clear precedent to follow, both the magistrate as well as the High Court failed in their duty to take corrective measures.

Section 124A has been a special weapon of choice for the administration in Kerala's neighbouring state, Tamil Nadu. In 2015, a singer by the name of Sivadas, also known as Kovan, was arrested for sedition for a song criticizing the chief minister Jayalalitha for the state government's support of for-profit liquor stores. He was also alleged to be a member of a Naxal organization. He was sent to police custody by a magistrate, against which he appealed before the Madras High Court. The High Court set aside the order of the magistrate on 7 November 2015 after finding no evidence of him being a member of any Naxal group. The state of Tamil Nadu filed an appeal against the High Court order, which was summarily dismissed by the Supreme Court on 30 November.[16] He is still facing sedition charges.

This action may be considered mild in comparison to what the Tamil Nadu government did about eight years back. It turned a coastal fishing village in Tamil Nadu into a village of sedition.

As Arun Janardhanan, a journalist with the *Indian Express*, calls it, the Idinthakarai village is ground zero on India's sedition map.[17] He reports that 8956 people from Idinthakarai and Kudankulam villages have been slapped with cases of sedition since 2011—the highest in India—because of their sustained protests against the commissioning of the coastal Kudankulam nuclear power plant, which was eventually commissioned in August 2016. Udayakumar, the second petitioner in the *Common Cause* petition,[18] is the de facto leader of the protests and the founder of the People's Movement against Nuclear Energy (PMANE), which was at the forefront of the protests.

The protests were a direct result of the Fukushima Daiichi nuclear plant accident which happened in Japan in March 2011. Following a major earthquake, a 15 metre tsunami disabled the power supply and cooling of three Fukushima Daiichi reactors, causing a nuclear accident which caused all three cores to melt in the first three days. Over 1,00,000 people were evacuated from their homes but according to official figures there have been well over 1000 deaths from maintaining the evacuation.[19]

With the doubts about the safety of the Kudankulam project, fears of a similar accident caused a mass protest which continues to this date, albeit more subdued. Almost 380 FIRs alleging sedition and waging war against the state were lodged against the protesters since October 2011 with Udayakumar as the first accused in many of them. Interestingly, the FIRs ended with the line 'and another 300' or '3,000 people' along with the name of the main accused. This was done to keep it open-ended and scare people into thinking that any of them could be implicated.

The Supreme Court on 6 May 2013 paved the way for the nuclear plant to be commissioned in Kudankulam as it found that the authorities had obtained all clearances and permissions and had implemented sufficient safety and security measures. It further held that the setting up of the Kudankulam plant would have positive effects on the welfare of the people and lead to economic growth. While issuing a wide array of directions, the Supreme Court ordered that endeavours should be made to withdraw all criminal cases filed against the agitators to restore peace and normalcy at Kudankulam and nearby places.[20]

However, according to Janardhanan's report, the number of cases dropped from 380 to 240, with twenty-one still standing as on the date of the report. The damage done by the cases was severe. Young men booked for sedition got their passports 'blacklisted' and had to give up their plans to go abroad to seek employment. Sundari, one of those arrested, served ninety-eight days in prison before getting conditional bail from the Madras High Court. She had to sign registers at three police stations in Madurai, more than 200 km away from her residence, every day for two months. After returning to her village, she had to sign the register at the Kudankulam police station each day for six more months.[21]

The most chilling statement on the sedition cases was made by an inspector general of the state police. He told Janardhanan, 'We write on the files "Further Action Dropped". But Kudankulam and Idinthakarai were most peculiar cases as we needed to keep a check on the villagers. Retaining these charges will help douse their anger; over 8000 people booked under charges will scare them to not initiate similar protests again.' Despite admitting that there was nothing to be probed or charge-sheeted in all these cases, the police officer said, 'These were all cases to scare them. When I look back after five years, I see that those 121 and 124A charges on 8000 random people did serve the purpose.'

Something similar occurred in Tamil Nadu in 2018, also in a coastal town called Thoothukudi. In a protest against the environmental issues arising from the smelting plant of Sterlite Copper, a Vedanta company, the town witnessed violence at a rally demanding the plant's closure. Ten people were killed in police firing and many injured. The Tamil Nadu police slapped hundreds of cases against the protestors, but the most unique case was filed against a lawyer providing legal aid to the arrested protestors. S. Vanchinathan, an advocate for the 'Thoothukudi District Anti-Sterlite People Federation' who practises at Madurai, was arrested on 20 June and kept in jail for sixteen days. He was booked for sedition and only granted bail on the condition that he remain in Madurai town and not engage in any activity related to Sterlite.[22]

The *Common Cause* petition was filed to prevent such cases in future, but the Supreme Court's order simply directing the application of *Kedar Nath* strictly would not help people like the Kudankulam protestors, who have had to suffer the side effects of sedition cases and live with the stigma of being called anti-nationals.

Like Arundhati Roy.

The Booker Prize–winning literary giant made a statement at a seminar called 'Azadi—the Only Way' held in Delhi on 21 October 2010. The seminar was held with a member of the separatist Hurriyat Conference of Kashmir present on stage with Roy. Recalling her past statements to the media, she said that Kashmir had never been an integral part of India and that India needed *azaadi* (freedom) from Kashmir as much as Kashmir needed azaadi from India.

She clarified by stating that by 'India' she did not mean the Indian State but the Indian people. She said, 'So, so many things have been done there, every time there's an election and people come out to vote, the Indian government goes and says—"Why do you want a referendum? There was a vote and the people have voted for India." . . . Now, sometimes it's very difficult to know from what place one stands on as formally a citizen of India, what can one say, what is one allowed to say, because when India was fighting for independence from British colonization—every argument that people now use to problematize the problems of azaadi in Kashmir were certainly used against Indians . . . I've seen and my heart is filled with appreciation for the struggle that people are waging, the fight that young people are fighting and I don't want them to be let down . . . I want to believe that this fight is a fight for justice . . . So I remember when I wrote in 2007, I said the one thing that broke my heart on the streets of Srinagar was when I heard people say "Nanga Bhooka Hindustan,[23] jaan se pyaara Pakistan".[24] I said, "No. Because the Nanga Bhooka Hindustan is with you. And if you're fighting for a just society then you must align yourselves with the powerless," . . . I hope that the young people will deepen their idea of Azaadi, it is something that the State and your enemies that you're fighting uses to divide you.'[25]

She concluded her speech by saying, 'Think about justice and don't pick and choose your injustices, don't say that "I want justice but it's okay if the next guy doesn't have it, or the next woman doesn't have it". Because justice is the keystone to integrity and integrity is the keystone to real resistance.' Her speech ruffled the feathers of both the then ruling United Progressive Alliance (UPA) government as well as the then opposition Bharatiya Janata Party (BJP), with calls made to book her for sedition.[26] However, the government subsequently decided not to do so as no case was made out against her.[27]

Arundhati Roy wears the stigma with pride, an option not available to the Kudankulam protestors. In the May 2016 issue of *Caravan* magazine, in an essay titled 'My Seditious Heart', Roy acknowledged the anti-national label that she carries, writing, 'Now it's true that my views on these matters are at variance with those of the ruling establishment. In better days, that used to be known as a critical perspective or an alternative worldview. These days in India, it's called sedition.'

Even someone like Arun Jaitley, the finance minister of India, could not escape sedition charges. Jaitley posted an article titled 'NJAC Judgment—an Alternative View' on his Facebook page in October 2015 which was critical of a Supreme Court judgment where a five-judge Constitution Bench of the court struck down the National Judicial Appointments Commission Act, 2014, and the Ninety-ninth Amendment to the Constitution as unconstitutional.

He wrote:

The judgment ignores the larger constitutional structure of India. Unquestionably, independence of the judiciary is a part of the basic structure of the Constitution. It needs to be preserved . . . The majority opinion was understandably concerned with one basic structure—independence of judiciary—but to rubbish all other basic structures by referring to them as 'politicians' and passing the judgment on a rationale that India's democracy has to be saved from its elected representatives. The Indian democracy cannot be a tyranny of the unelected and if the elected are undermined, democracy itself would be in danger . . . No principle of interpretation of law anywhere in the world, gives the judicial institutions the jurisdiction to interpret a constitutional provision to mean the opposite of what the Constituent Assembly had said. This is the second fundamental error in the judgment. The court can only interpret—it cannot be the third chamber of the legislature to rewrite a law . . . I believe that the two can and must co-exist. Independence of the judiciary is an important basic structure of the Constitution. To strengthen it, one does not have to weaken Parliamentary sovereignty which is not only an essential basic structure but is the soul of our democracy.[28]

A magistrate in Mahoba district in Uttar Pradesh *suo moto*— meaning on his own initiative—decided to register a sedition case and issued summons against Jaitley, ridiculously claiming that no citizen has a right to disrespect any pillar of democracy and cannot question an order of a court. He completely ignored the legal mandate that any offence under Section 124A of the IPC can only be taken cognizance of after prior approval of the government, as required under Section 196 of the Criminal Procedure Code. The Allahabad High Court quashed the complaint and the summons against Jaitley, holding that none of the ingredients of Section 124A were met, apart from there being a procedural irregularity. It lambasted the magistrate for not applying its judicial mind and for acting irresponsibly.

The Court said, 'The initiation of criminal prosecution has serious consequences. It relates to the life and liberty of a citizen and carries with it grave consequences. Viewed in that light it is obvious that the exercise of power by the Magistrate must be preceded by due application of mind and circumspection.'[29]

The High Court's intervention in Jaitley's case only highlighted the lack of judicial protection in the Tamil Nadu and Kerala cases, and the inefficacy of the Supreme Court's direction in the *Common Cause* case.

In fact, the Karnataka High court recently dismissed the anticipatory bail application of the administrator of a WhatsApp group in which some group members had shared 'Pakistan zindabad'[30] slogans. A case for sedition was registered on the basis alleging that one person had posted a slogan stating 'Pakistan zindabad' on 14 August 2018. The accused approached the High Court for anticipatory bail where the state police opposed it alleging that the slogan provoked the public at large to raise communal violence against different classes and the act amounted to sedition.

The High Court while rejecting the bail application observed that, 'It is necessary to state that the slogan may be of one line or two lines but the intention and effect when observed is grievous.'[31]

The Court clearly abdicated its responsibility in this matter, which was against the precedent set down by the Supreme Court in the *Kedar Nath, Balwant Singh* and *Bilal Ahmad* cases. It also highlights the mechanical approach the police take in such cases. It didn't help that the accused were members of the minority community.

Like in the case of Saleem, who had come to the Chennai airport to receive a friend. He was arrested by the airport police and a FIR was registered against him simply for receiving a message on his phone which was an appeal for Muslims to gather at Delhi's Jantar Mantar for a 'show of strength'. He was arrested for indulging in anti-national activities even though he was just the recipient of the message, which in itself was innocuous, and by no stretch of the imagination hinted towards incitement of violence or public disorder. A magistrate, however, released him after not finding any criminality in the matter.[32]

Criticizing a Supreme Court judgment on Facebook got Jaitley into trouble, for which the Allahabad High Court had to come to his rescue. Kamal Shukla, a journalist in Chhattisgarh, lampooned the Supreme Court's judgment[33] in the case, calling for a probe into the mysterious death of B.H. Loya, a judge hearing the Sohrabuddin encounter trial, which had occurred in December 2014. He published a cartoon on his Facebook page criticizing the judgment which somehow offended a person sitting in Rajasthan. Shukla, an editor of the regional weekly *Bhumakal Samachar,* was arrested in April for sedition based on the complaint. He is currently out on bail with no one coming to his rescue.[34]

Another journalist, this time in Manipur, was arrested for sedition on 21 November 2018 for posting a video critical of Manipur Chief Minister N. Biren Singh and Prime Minister Narendra Modi on Facebook. Kishorechandra Wangkhem had posted a video criticizing Biren Singh and calling him a 'puppet of Modi and Hindutva' for organizing a function in Manipur on 19 November to mark the birth anniversary of Rani Lakshmibai of Jhansi, who he claimed had no significance for Manipur. He questioned the chief minister's sense of 'Manipuri nationalism' and used expletives for Modi and Singh. He dared the police to arrest him, which they duly obliged him with. However, the chief judicial magistrate threw out the charges and observed, 'In giving the speech, the accused person transgressed beyond decent human conduct but it cannot be termed seditious . . . The government, especially its functionary like prime minister cannot be so sensitive as to take offence upon expression of opinions by its citizen, which may be given very nicely by using proper words or indecently by using some vulgar terms.'[35]

Having failed to book him for sedition, the state government detained him under the National Security Act,

1980 which enables the state to arrest someone as preventive detention for a period up to a year!

Closely following on the heels of Wangkhem's sedition charge, the protests in Assam against the Citizenship (Amendment) Bill, 2019 resulted in sedition charges against another journalist and two other civil society members. The Bill proposes that persons belonging to minority communities, namely, Hindus, Sikhs, Buddhists, Jains, Parsis and Christians from Afghanistan, Bangladesh and Pakistan, shall not be treated as illegal migrants. The Lok Sabha passed the Bill on 8 January 2019, which provoked protests across Assam based on the fear of influx of immigrants from Bangladesh, and the naturalization of illegal immigrants already in the state.

Senior journalist Manjit Mahanta, Sahitya Akademi awardee litterateur Hiren Gohain and RTI activist Akhil Gogoi were charged with sedition for their comments on the Citizenship Bill at an event held on 7 January 2019 organized by a civil society group. Gohain was alleged to have called for an 'independent Assam'. He contradicted the police's story and claimed that he had only highlighted that citizenship should be on the basis of secular principles, and the demands of the Assamese people on the Citizenship Bill must be achieved by democratic means within the framework of the Constitution. He claims to have stated that a failure to do so would lead to demands for an independent Assam.[36] Gogoi and Mahanta also denied the allegations and claimed to have made statements similar to Gohain, that failure to meet Assamese demands against the Bill may lead to a situation where people might start demanding an independent Assam.[37]

All three filed a petition for pre-arrest bail before the Guwahati High Court, which granted such bail to Mahanta, albeit conditional, but only granted interim pre-arrest bail to Gohain and Gogoi on 11 January.[38] At the time of writing this, the petition was still pending before the High Court with investigations ongoing.

Meanwhile, after having been passed by the Lok Sabha, the Citizenship (Amendment) Bill was not tabled in the Rajya Sabha till the last day of the Parliamentary session on 13 February despite being listed for consideration. The Bill has now lapsed and will have to be reintroduced in the Lok Sabha in the next session, if at all.[39]

However, this did not stop the Manipur police from arresting a Manipuri student leader for sedition for his statements against the Bill. Thokchom Veewon was arrested from his home in Delhi in a joint operation between the Manipur and Delhi police on the evening of 15 February 2019. The Manipur police charged him with sedition for a Facebook post criticizing the Bill on 12 February in which he called the chief minister of Manipur a puppet of the central government.

The police, meanwhile, claim that Veewon was booked for sedition for his call for Manipuri independence, and not for his criticism of the chief minister. In another post he had written, 'Indefinite curfew imposed in Manipur. Internet banned for 5 days. All cable TV network asked not to cover any speech or footage of the protest. High possibility that CAB will be passed today at the Rajya Sabha. Manipur once burned down the state assembly in 2001. Self determination is the only way forward.' An inquiry by the Criminal Investigation Department of the crime branch of the Manipur police led to a report based on which the sedition case was filed against Veewon in an Imphal police station as FIR No. 13(2)2019 LLI-PS. A magistrate in Delhi permitted the Manipur police to take Veewon to Imphal to face further proceedings. This permission, known as a transit remand, was challenged before the Delhi High Court by his brother. The High Court not only refused to interfere with the transit remand, it went ahead to give a finding that Veewon prima facie appeared to have committed the offence of sedition. It quickly qualified the finding by saying that it had not commented on the merits of the case.[40] The order of the High Court appears mechanical and suffers from a lack of appreciation of the law. Veewon's family, however, decided to face proceedings in Manipur instead of challenging the High Court's order before the Supreme Court.

The magistrate before whom Veewon was subsequently produced proved to be a bigger champion of free speech than the Delhi High Court. She granted him bail after prima facie finding that the offence of sedition did not appear to have been committed.[41] She is the same magistrate who had earlier rescued Wangkhem from sedition charges.

The need to prosecute Veewon for sedition makes little sense because now that the Bill has lapsed there is no fear of imminent violence or public disorder. The comments made by Veewon are similar to the statements made by Gohain and others in Assam which can be interpreted as a caution against disturbing status quo in the region. Would such calls by a student leader spark disaffection and hatred against the government and lead to violence and disorder? There is no need to even guess because even after his posts no such unlawful events occurred, neither is there any possibility of such acts now.

The police may have arrested Veewon to send a statement to people in the region that opposition to the government will not be tolerated. The arrest of civil society members in Assam and Manipur is a message to the people across the north-east that anyone against the actions of the government would have to face serious consequences. The law against sedition and other offences against the State is being wielded by the police as a baton to crush dissent and put the fear of the law in the minds of people. In Assam alone, 251 sedition cases have been filed since 26 May 2016, which was the day the current BJP government came to power in the state.[42]

Despite the Supreme Court clarifying the law of sedition on multiple occasions now, law enforcement authorities are yet to understand what the law actually means. Or even worse, as demonstrated by past actions, they understand what it means but still initiate prosecutions and leave the rest up to the courts. The police in India have rarely been held accountable for such detentions and arrests, which has further emboldened them to flout Supreme Court guidelines and misapply the law. In a fractured society, more than the law against sociopolitical offences, it is the law enforcement authorities which are a bigger threat against free speech and political freedoms.

A senior police officer in Jharkhand lamented the lack of understanding of the sedition law among lower-rung police officers in the state. The police in Jharkhand are national leaders in registering sedition cases, mostly against alleged Maoist insurgents or sympathizers, but all these cases fell flat at the first hint of legal scrutiny. In many cases, charge sheets were filed only to be rejected as no prior approval under Section 196 of the Criminal Procedure Code had been taken. This was down to the fact that the police were not even aware of this legal requirement![43]

Recently, as admitted by the state government, about 250 people were charged with sedition in the Khunti district of Jharkhand in twenty-three separate cases. Tribal leaders and activists claimed that the actual number is as high as 1500 people. The cases have arisen from the Pathalgarhi movement in the district, which refers to a traditional tribal way to mark territory and jurisdiction by the erection of stone slabs. In this instance, stone slabs with the relevant provisions of law were erected in the district, claiming that no government activity could be undertaken in the area without permission from the *gram sabha* or village assembly. The government has interpreted this as a move to hinder developmental work.[44]

The villagers do have a point. The Supreme Court, by way of the *Samatha* judgment, declared that Scheduled Tribe lands, as specified in accordance with Schedule V of the Constitution, cannot be transferred to non-tribal persons or corporations, and recognized the rights of indigenous persons over such forests and land. Additionally, the Panchayats (Extension to Scheduled Areas) Act, 1996 establishes their rights over exploitation of resources and self-governance in Scheduled Tribe areas. Activists claim that the Jharkhand government has been attempting to bypass provisions of law, like taking gram sabha approval for projects in the area, resulting in the Pathalgarhi movement in Khunti.[45]

Sedition cases have also been registered against tribal rights activists involved with the movement who consequently filed a petition before the Jharkhand High Court in September 2018 seeking quashing of the charges. The petition is still pending adjudication.[46]

The most interesting recent sedition case also originates from Jharkhand. This case has its origin in the creation of the autonomous South-West Frontier Province of Bengal, which included the Kolhan region which is now in Jharkhand. This region was technically not a part of British India. The British followed a policy of non-regulation of the indigenous tribes there, and the tribes had their own societal and political structures. The region was administered by a British resident named Wilkinson, who was more of a peacekeeper and go-between with the British administration.[47]

In 1982–83, a group of leaders from the region, under the banner of the Kolhan Raksha Sangh, travelled to

London demanding a separate independent state called 'Kolhan Estate Government', as it had purportedly been a region separate from India. They even demanded the right to interact with the Commonwealth on their own. They were duly booked for sedition. The movement again gained some steam a couple of years back with a group of tribals demanding independence citing the British-era arrangement. Their leader, an octogenarian ex-additional district magistrate of undivided Bihar,[48] Ramo Birua, had issued a call to hoist the flag for a separate Kolhan Estate Government and had begun issuing certificates for caste, income and age under the letterhead of 'Kolhan Estate Government'. He was booked for sedition, after which he went underground.[49]

Birua was finally arrested in June 2018, having evaded the law by hiding in a jungle, and was later sheltered by his children. He was eighty-four years old when he was arrested.

He died of natural causes twenty days later.

11

The Road Ahead

As mentioned earlier, the National Crime Records Bureau (NCRB) started maintaining a separate record of sedition cases in India from the year 2014. A total forty-seven cases of sedition under Section 124A of the IPC were registered in the year 2014 for which fifty-eight people were arrested. In 2015, it decreased to thirty cases with seventy-three people arrested, but increased to thirty-five FIRs in 2016 with forty-eight arrests. By the end of 2016, sixty-one sedition cases were still pending investigation. No official NCRB data is available post-2016 as the NCRB has not released any reports after that.

At the end of 2016, only sixteen cases reached the charge-sheet stage. As per the report, thirty-four trials for sedition were conducted in 2016, out of which only three cases were concluded, resulting in a single conviction and two acquittals. This report has also been presented in Parliament by the minister of state for home affairs on 15 March 2016. The table accompanying the written answer submitted by the minister notes the only conviction to be in Jharkhand. However, media reports claim that there have been two convictions for sedition since 2014. One in Jharkhand in 2014 and one in Andhra Pradesh in 2016.[1]

I tried to test the data, but despite trawling through court records in the relevant districts and High Courts in Jharkhand and Andhra Pradesh, one could not find a record of even a single conviction in either state. Usually, such convictions find their way to the press, but even local or national newspapers did not contain any reports about sedition convictions during the relevant time period. This raises doubts about the NCRB data for 2016, which records one conviction, as well as press reports which claim that two convictions took place from 2014 to 2016.

So, I dug deeper. The basis of most press reports claiming two convictions seems to be data from the Home Ministry, which notes two convictions. This is in variance with the official NCRB data and the table submitted in Parliament by the ministry. I made inquiries through local officials in Jharkhand and Andhra Pradesh and was reliably told that there is no record of any conviction under Section 124A in either state.

Something, somewhere, broke in the recording and reporting process, and it seems to be down to a clerical error, maybe, that the NCRB and the ministry got it wrong. Therefore, it appears that there has not been even a single conviction under Section 124A of the IPC in the three years since 2014, for which records are available. At the time of writing this, the NCRB had not released the data for 2017 and 2018.

The Law Commission of India undertook the task of revising the Indian Penal Code in 1968 and came up with a report in 1971.[2] The Commission was of the view that the language of Section 124A was defective as 'the pernicious tendency or intention' underlying seditious words or utterances has not been expressly related to the interest of the security or integrity of India or of public order as provided under Article 19(2) of the Constitution. The commission suggested that this could be rectified by specifically introducing the aspect of *mens rea*, meaning criminal intention, in Section 124A. In other words, it wanted the provision to be very clear that only speeches or writings delivered with the specific intent and knowledge that they would endanger the integrity or security of India or any state or disturb public order would be considered seditious.

On the other hand, it was also in favour of expanding the scope of the provision to penalize disaffection against the Constitution, the legislatures and the judiciary in addition to the executive. Fortunately, the government of the day did not accept the recommendations made in this regard. Unfortunately, it also did not accept the recommendation to specifically include the aspect of *mens rea* in Section 124A.

Interestingly, the birthplace of the common law of sedition has already abolished the law. Section 73 of the Coroners and Justice Act, 2009 categorically abolished the common law offences of sedition and seditious libel in England, Wales and Northern Ireland. In doing so, the legislature recognized that the law of sedition had a chilling effect on free speech and political discourse and debate. Speaking on the abolition, Justice Minister Claire Ward said, 'Sedition and seditious and defamatory libel are arcane offences—from a bygone era when freedom of expression wasn't seen as the right it is today. Freedom of speech is now seen as the touchstone of democracy, and the ability of individuals to criticise the state is crucial to maintaining freedom. The existence of these obsolete offences in this country had been used by other countries as justification for the retention of similar laws which have been actively used to suppress political dissent and restrict press freedom. Abolishing these offences will allow the UK to take a lead in challenging similar laws in other countries, where they are used to suppress free speech.'[3]

This statement becomes more significant in the Indian context. The offence as described under Section 124A of the IPC has been carried forward from colonial days and is very broadly worded. It reads as a preventive provision which should ideally be used only as an emergency measure. A more specific law was enacted in 1967 by Parliament to impose reasonable restrictions on freedom of speech in the interests of sovereignty and integrity of India pursuant to the sixteenth amendment of the Constitution in 1963. The Unlawful Activities (Prevention) Act, 1967 (UAPA) received the assent of the president on 30 December 1967.

UAPA defines 'unlawful activity' as any action undertaken by an individual or association through words, either written or spoken, or through signs or visible representation that (a) intends, or supports any claim, to cession or secession of any territory which forms a part of India, or incites other people to do so; (b) intends to or disclaims, questions, disrupts the territorial integrity and sovereignty of India; and (c) causes or intends to cause disaffection against India. The definition clearly covers, and even expands, the provision under Section 124A. Section 13 of the UAPA provides the punishment for unlawful activities and states that whoever commits, advocates, abets, advises or incites the commission of any unlawful activity shall be punished with imprisonment for up to seven years, or a fine, or both.

The continued existence of Section 124A, despite the presence of the UAPA governing this special category of offences against the State, makes little sense under the circumstances. There are problems with the UAPA as well, especially with the width of language employed to define unlawful activity, which penalizes even passive support or advocacy of a political issue which may be considered to be an unlawful activity.

The Rowlatt Act, despite all its unpopularity, did provide that measures against seditious activities can only be invoked upon a declaration of emergency by the government of the day. The UAPA was enacted during a period when India had emerged from major wars with China and Pakistan, and the government anticipated more such conflicts due to the geopolitical environment at the time. Section 124A was enacted at the time of Wahhabi extremism and was subsequently used to suppress freedom movements. Today, the nation is not under threat of war or any major conflict. God forbid, if such a situation does arise, then the government can always declare it expedient to apply Section 124A or the UAPA to deal with emergent circumstances. Even to tackle internal security problems like the Maoist insurgency in the states of Jharkhand, Chhattisgarh, Odisha, Andhra Pradesh, etc., or the separatist insurgency in the north-east and Kashmir, the law against sedition can be applied only to such notified regions which are affected by the problem. Any such notification must be based on sound evidence and reasons for the application of Section 124A or UAPA.

However, it will serve democracy well to repeal Section 124A of the IPC and instead rely on UAPA only upon a declaration of emergency. India is not a brittle democracy that needs protection from undesirable speech or expression in times of peace.

For these very reasons, D. Raja, a member of the Rajya Sabha in 2011, introduced a private member's bill to repeal Section 124A. It was called the Indian Penal Code (Amendment) Bill, 2011 which proposed an unconditional abolition of sedition law due to the presence of alternative legislation. In support of his Bill, Raja stated:

In view of the adverse effect of the section on individuals and organizations that work for unity, integrity, and equitable development of India and its citizens, it is felt necessary to delete section 124A from the Indian Penal Code, 1860. In the State of Chhattisgarh, many people, human rights activists and social activists, who have been working amongst the tribal people for their upliftment, were targeted, booked and imprisoned under this clause. My question is that why should it happen? In several other States also this clause has been continuously misused to suppress genuine people's movement and the individuals who voice the concerns of our people. Even in the States like Haryana and Punjab, people who have been fighting for the rights of agricultural workers, for the rights of dalits, they have been targeted. Even the people who are critical of nuclear plants, the nuclear policy they are targeted. There should be demarcation. I do not agree the way the neo-liberal economic policies are pursued with such aggressiveness. I have the right to question the government. You cannot use section 124A of the Indian Penal Code against your own citizens. As a sovereign nation we should really think whether we should keep this section. It is the duty of the Government to safeguard the interests of tribal people. What is the necessity of section 124A in the Indian Penal Code? When somebody questions the Nuclear Policy or when somebody opposes nuclear plants, the State machinery comes down so heavily. We should amend the Indian Penal Code. This section is being misused mostly against those activists and organizations who are basically working among the poorest of our people. Do you believe that there is a need to have this section even after six decades of Independence? Have you ever thought of using this section against tax evaders? This section is used precisely against those who fight for the welfare of the people. I want to emphasise the need for deletion of this clause. It is a draconian clause. It has to go. It is the question of defending the Fundamental Rights of the Indian citizens. If you continue to have this clause, the Government fails to uphold the Constitutional provisions. This Clause is used as a weapon against people who fight against the Government's policies.[4]

The government justified the continued existence of Section 124A by relying on the Law Commission's 42nd report, which recommended the strengthening of Section 124A. The minister of state for home affairs replied to D. Raja by stating:

During the last 61 years of Republic of India, no Government deleted this section because this section certainly strengthens the authority of the State. It is essential to have a strong State to safeguard the democratic set up. Section 124A of IPC is absolutely compatible with democracy. The number of cases in respect of section 124A could be even less and very negligible. We cannot delete the section 124 A of the IPC on the mere apprehension that there are chances of its misuse. There is no harm in reviewing the provisions of this section to make it more in tune with the present day need of the civil society and freedom of speech and expression. The Government recognises the imperative need to reform the criminal justice system of the country by introducing a comprehensive legislation in Parliament. In view of the recommendations of the Department-related Parliamentary Standing Committee on Home Affairs, the Ministry of Home Affairs requested the Ministry of law and Justice to request the Law Commission of India to examine and give a comprehensive report covering all aspects of criminal law so that comprehensive amendments can be made in various laws. The Report of the Law Commission of India in this regard is awaited. Considering all these facts, I request my hon. Friend, Mr. D. Raja, to kindly withdraw this Bill.

Assured by the government's reply, D. Raja withdrew the private member's bill.[5]

Another attempt to amend the provision was made through a separate private member's bill introduced by Shashi Tharoor in the Lok Sabha called the Indian Penal Code (Amendment) Bill, 2015. Through this Bill, Tharoor lamented the inefficacy of the Supreme Court's judgment in *Kedar Nath* as lower judiciary and law enforcement agencies continued to misapply the law against sedition. The trigger for the Bill was the imposition of sedition charges against the Kudankulam protestors. He called for amendment of the provision to clearly lay down what the Supreme Court read into the provision in the judgment. However, even this attempt did not bear fruit.

On 30 August 2018, the 21st Law Commission of India published a consultation paper seeking public views and recommendations regarding Section 124A of the IPC. The Commission was of the view that in a democratic society every irresponsible exercise of the right to free speech and expression cannot be termed seditious, and if the country is not open to positive criticism, there lies little difference between the pre-

and post-Independence eras. It felt that while it is essential to protect national integrity, sedition law should not be misused as a tool to curb free speech because dissent and criticism are essential ingredients of a vibrant democracy.

Therefore, in order to consider revising Section 124A, the commission framed the following propositions, as extracted from the consultation paper:

(i) The United Kingdom abolished sedition laws ten years back citing that the country did not want to be quoted as an example of using such draconian laws. Given the fact that the section itself was introduced by the British to use as a tool to oppress the Indians, how far it is justified to retain Section 124A in the Penal Code?

(ii) Should sedition be not redefined in a country like India—the largest democracy of the world—considering that right to free speech and expression is an essential ingredient of democracy ensured as a Fundamental Right by our Constitution?

(iii) Will it be worthwhile to think of an option of renaming the section with a suitable substitute for the term sedition and prescribe punishment accordingly?

(iv) What is the extent to which the citizens of our country may enjoy the right to offend?

(v) At what point the right to offend would qualify as hate speech?

(vi) How to strike a balance between Section 124A and right to freedom of speech and expression?

(vii) In view of the fact that there are several statutes which take care of various acts which were earlier considered seditious, how far would keeping Section 124A in the Penal Code, serve any purpose?

(viii) Given the fact that all the existing statutes cover the various offences against the individual and/or the offences against the society, will reducing the rigour of Section 124A or repealing it be detrimental or beneficial, to the nation?

(ix) In a country, where contempt of Court invites penal action, should contempt against the Government established by law not invite punishment?

(x) What could be the possible safeguards to ensure that section 124A is not misused?

The Commission invited views from legal luminaries, lawmakers, government and non-government agencies, academia, students and the general public on the propositions to enable it to recommend appropriate measures to the government. Unfortunately, the term of the 21st Law Commission ended in August 2018 itself.

The constitution of the 22nd Law Commission is still awaited.

Notes

Chapter 1: Company Raj

1. Bipan Chandra, *History of Modern India* (New Delhi: Orient BlackSwan, 2009).
2. Arthur Berriedale Keith, *A Constitutional History of India, 1600–1935* (London: Methuen and Co., 1936).
3. John William Kaye, *The Administration of the East India Company* (London: Richard Bentley, 1853).
4. M.P. Jain, *Indian Legal History* (Nagpur: Wadhwa and Co., 2006).
5. Amar Farooqui, *The Establishment of British Rule, 1757–1813: A People's History of India, Vol. 23* (New Delhi: Tulika Books, 2014).
6. Present-day Kanyakumari in Tamil Nadu.
7. Kaye, *The Administration of the East India Company*.
8. Keith, *A Constitutional History of India, 1600–1935*.
9. Jain, *Indian Legal History*.
10. Kaye, *The Administration of the East India Company*.
11. Keith, *A Constitutional History of India, 1600–1935*.
12. Jain, *Indian Legal History*.
13. Chandra, *History of Modern India*.

14. Present-day Bharuch in Gujarat.

15. Present-day Machilipatnam in Andhra Pradesh.

16. Mina Choudhuri and Mrinmaya Choudhuri, *Glimpses of the Justice of Presidency Towns, 1687–1973* (New Delhi: Regency Publications, 2006).

17. Peter Auber, *Constitution of the East India Company* (London: Kingsbury Parbury and Allen, 1826).

18. Present-day Madras in Tamil Nadu.

19. Edgar Thurston, *The Madras Presidency* (Cambridge: Cambridge University Press, 1913).

20. Edmund C. Cox, *Short History of Bombay Presidency* (Thacker & Co., 1887).

21. Lillias C. Davidson, *Catherine of Braganza* (London: John Murray, 1908).

22. James Grant, *Cassell's Illustrated History of India* (London: Cassell Petter & Galpin, 1880).

23. James Mill, *The History of British India* (London: Baldwin Cradock & Joy, 1817).

24. Chandra, *History of Modern India*.

25. Decided on 10 May 1943, reported as (1945) 47 BOMLR 525.

26. Jain, *Indian Legal History*.

27. Pitt's India Act, 1784.

28. Keith, *A Constitutional History of India, 1600–1935*.

29. C.H. Philips, *The Secret Committee of the East India Company, 1784–1858* (London: Bulletin of the SOAS, 1940).

30. Hindu scriptures.

31. D.A. Washbrook, 'Law, State and Agrarian Society in Colonial India', *Modern Asian Studies* 15.3 (1981): 649–721.

32. Marc Galanter, 'Displacement of Traditional Law in Modern India', *Journal of Social Issues* 24.4 (1968).

33. Sir Henry Maine, member of the governor general's council (1863–69).

Chapter 2: Bentham, Mill and Macaulay

1. The account of Nanda Kumar's trial is based mainly on *The Trial of Maharaja Nand Kumar* by Henry Beveridge (Thacker, Spink & Co., 1886) and *The Story of Nuncomar* by James F. Stephen (Macmillan & Co., 1885). Beveridge's book was written as a response to Stephen's book as he felt that Stephen was biased towards holding that Hastings and Impey were not at fault. Stephen had in his book raised doubts on essays on the trial written earlier by Beveridge. More than that, Stephen had stated that Beveridge was not that proficient in English law. Beveridge, who was a judge of the High Court at Calcutta, took it personally and felt the need to respond by calling Nanda Kumar's trial and execution a judicial murder. In his book dedication, Beveridge writes, 'I dedicate this to my wife who has taken so much interest in the attempt to vindicate a persecuted Bengali.' Interestingly, Stephen had felt a need to write his book partly in response to Thomas Macaulay who in his essay on Warren Hastings was scathing in criticism of the Nanda Kumar trial, and also considered it a judicial murder. A more recent account of the Nanda Kumar story has been provided by A.G. Noorani in *Indian Political Trials* (Oxford University Press, 2005).
2. Hastings was facing immense scrutiny from some members of the English Parliament and thus Nanda Kumar's demise was a reprieve for him.
3. English barrister who was an advocate for abolition of capital punishment.

4. Phil Handler, 'Forgery and the End of the "Bloody Code" in Early Nineteenth Century England', *Historical Journal* 48 (2005).

5. *Mason v. State*, 206 SW 3d 869 (2005).

6. Bentham's life and works are written about in the book *Jeremy Bentham: His Life and Works* by Charles M. Atkinson (Methuen & Co., 1905).

7. An Inn was, loosely, an association of which Barristers are members and in the old days provided lodgings for them. Even today, initiation into such Inns is referred to as 'eating dinner' at the Inn, which was literally the case in the old days. Lincoln's Inn was one the most prominent Inns of Court for English barristers. More about Lincoln's Inn can be read at www.lincolnsinn.org.uk.

8. Bentham, in his first notable work published in 1776, called *A Fragment of Government*, heavily criticized the commentaries of Blackstone. However, the book was published as the work of an anonymous author at the time, considering the unpopularity of the principles of utility.

9. Bentham published *An Introduction to the Principles of Morals and Legislation* in 1789, which was a compendium of all his writings on the subject, including a chapter on 'General Principles of Legislation'.

10. Bentham was later very unhappy with some consequences of the French Revolution.

11. Also known as Stephen Dumont, a Swiss, he was a friend of Bentham's and the editor of Bentham's works.

12. English translation of the title.

13. Alexander Bain wrote *James Mill: A Biography* (Longman, Green & Co., 1882). Bain's motive behind painstakingly piecing together the biography was that he had failed to come across a proper account of Mill's life, who in his estimation was one of the greater characters in contemporary British history.

14. The Charter of 1813.

15. The summary of the Act is based on the text of 'A Bill for Effecting an Arrangement with the India Company, and for the Better Government of His Majesty's Indian Territories' which formed part of *Further Papers Respecting the East India Company's Charter* published in 1833 by Cox and Son by order of the general court for the information of the proprietors of the East India Company. The papers contain minutes of the meetings of the secret committee of the East India Company and correspondence between the directors, Indian officials of the Company, members of the British Parliament, ministers in the government and the Board of Control. The papers shed light on the negotiations and representations which led to the enactment of the Charter Act of 1833 and evidences the East India Company's resistance to the Charter and their attempts to hold on to their only remaining trade monopoly, which was over trade of tea and opium, etc., from China. The resolute Parliament did not succumb to the Company's resistance in the face of the opposition of traders and the public to the trading nature of the Company. Therefore, it is safe to say that the East India Company was not very popular with British traders and citizens at that point of time.

16. George P. Landlow, 'The British East India Company—the Company That Owned a Nation (or Two)', www.victorianweb.org (accessed 15 August 2018).

17. Keith, *A Constitutional History of India, 1600–1935*.

18. Macaulay's speech was delivered on 10 July 1833 in the House of Commons when the Bill to enact the Charter was placed before Parliament for a second reading. The motion was carried out without a division but only after a long debate during which Macaulay delivered his famous speech. 'Government of India' delivered in the British

Parliament by Macaulay on 10 July 1833, which I have referenced at footnote no. 18. Complete Works of Lord Macaulay published by G.B. Putnam's Sons in 1898.

19. Macaulay mentioned this in a letter dated 21 October 1833 which he wrote to his sister Hannah M. Macaulay, who eventually accompanied him to India in 1834. Macaulay's letters have been published by his nephew George Otto Trevelyan in the book *The Life and Letters of Lord Macaulay* (1877).

20. Bain, *James Mill: A Biography*. On Mill's death in 1836, Macaulay wrote that he was a sincere mourner for Mill and had been on the best of terms with him. He mentioned that he had even received a very kind letter from Mill a week before his death.

21. Letter from Macaulay to Lord Lansdowne dated 5 December 1833. Macaulay was paid 10,000 pounds a year for his work in India, which was nothing short of a king's ransom at that time.

22. The Institutes of Hindu Law refers to the Ordinances of *Manu* (the first man according to various Hindu texts) or the *Manusmriti*. There are over fifty texts of the *Manusmriti* which are also known as the *Manava Dharmshastra*.

23. Macaulay believed that the process of codification should be driven by a small group of veteran jurists instead of democratic assemblies. His reasoning was that a small benevolent but despotic group would be more efficient than a democratic legislature that entails protracted debate which causes delay.

Chapter 3: The Indian Penal Code and Sedition

1. George Otto Trevelyan, *The Life and Letters of Lord Macaulay* (New York: Harper & Brothers, 1877).

2. A state within the United States of America.
3. The background of the draft IPC is explained in the Introductory Report submitted along with the draft code.
4. Term for territories within the presidencies beyond the towns of Calcutta, Bombay and Madras.
5. The draft penal code was published by the orders of the governor general in 1837 by G.H. Huttmann at the Bengal Military Orphan Press.
6. Not in any particular order. Macaulay wrote very detailed notes on each chapter (numbering from A to R) which were annexed to the introductory report to the draft Indian Penal Code.
7. John D. Mayne, *Criminal Law of India* (Higginbotham & Co., 1896). This book was also published at the same time by Thacker & Co. in Bombay, Thacker, Spink & Co. in Calcutta and W.M. Clowes & Sons in London.
8. James F. Stephen's commentary *The History of Criminal Law of England* published in three volumes by Macmillan & Co. in 1883 sheds light on the history and status of the law of sedition in England.
9. From the French region of Normandy which invaded England in the eleventh century.
10. From the Germanic region of Denmark and North Germany.
11. The originals inhabitants of England when the Roman conquest made it a part of the Roman Empire.
12. The ascension and rule of King Edward I has been recorded in *The Life and Reign of King Edward I* written by Edmund Clifford and published by Seeley, Jackson & Halliday in 1872.
13. Stephen, *The History of Criminal Law of England.*
14. Ibid.
15. Ibid.
16. Ibid.

17. Atul Chandra Patra, 'An Historical Introduction to the Indian Penal Code', *Journal of the Indian Law Institute* 3.3 (1961).

18. J.E.D. Bethune (1801–51) was also the president of the Council of Education and founded the first school for girls called the Hindu Female School in Calcutta in 1849, which was later called the Bethune School. The school eventually developed into a college and is now known as the Bethune College, http://www.bethunecollege.ac.in/BethuneCollege/BethuneCollege.htm (accessed 25 August 2018).

19. Eric Stokes, *The English Utilitarians and India* (Oxford University Press, 1959).

20. Chandra, *History of Modern India*.

21. Part of present-day Uttar Pradesh.

22. R.C. Majumdar wrote *The Sepoy Mutiny and the Revolt of 1857* (Kolkata: Calcutta Oriental Press, 1957) in the centenary year of the revolt, at the same time as when the Indian government published the official account of the revolt. He has explained in detail the causes of the revolt based on published accounts from historians and witnesses.

23. In present-day West Bengal.

24. Bahadur Shah had parlayed with the British to spare his and his family's life. However, the day after his surrender an officer by the name of Hodson massacred the princes after arresting them from Humayun's Tomb in Delhi.

25. Keith, *A Constitutional History of India, 1600–1935*.

26. Stephen, *The History of Criminal Law of England*.

27. A Legislative Council which was to be headed by the Legislative Member of the Governor General's Council was created by the Charter Act of 1853 to replace the structure existing under the Charter Act of 1833.

28. As per Section 1 of the IPC, 1860, as originally enacted.

29. Patra, 'An Historical Introduction to the Indian Penal Code'.
30. Trevelyan, *The Life and Letters of Lord Macaulay*.
31. Stephen, *The History of Criminal Law of England*.
32. Trevelyan, *The Life and Letters of Lord Macaulay*.
33. Leslie Stephen, *The Life of Sir James Fitzjames Stephen* (Smith Elder & Co., 1895). Leslie Stephen was the younger brother of James F. Stephen.
34. Stephen, *The History of Criminal Law of England*.
35. Clause 3 of the State Offences Act of 1857.
36. Clause 4 of the State Offences Act of 1857.
37. Clause 6 of the State Offences Act of 1857.
38. Present-day Uttar Pradesh.
39. Capital city of the state of Bihar.
40. The region between present-day Indian Punjab and Afghanistan.
41. A city in present-day Haryana.
42. Qeyamuddin Ahmad, *The Wahabi Movement in India* (Firma K.L. Mukhopadhyay, 1966).
43. Aravind Ganachari, *Nationalism and Social Reform in a Colonial Situation* (Kalpaz Publications, 2004).
44. *Reg. v. Sullivan* cited as 11 Cox 45.
45. Walter Russell Donogh, *A Treatise on the Law of Sedition and Cognate Offences in British India* (Thacker, Spink & Co., 1911).
46. Section 9 of the Dramatic Performances Act of 1876.
47. Ibid.

Chapter 4: Four Trials and an Amendment

1. Founded in 1875 by Dayanand Saraswati in Bombay.
2. Founded in 1828 by Raja Ram Mohan Roy and Debendranath Tagore in Calcutta.
3. Festival.

4. Self-rule.

5. Locally manufactured.

6. R.C. Majumdar, *History of the Freedom Movement in India* (Firma K.L. Mukhopadhyay, 1962).

7. Ibid.

8. Ibid.

9. B. Pattabhi Sitaramayya, *The History of the Indian National Congress (1885–1935),* published by the Working Committee of the Indian National Congress in 1935 on the occasion of its fiftieth anniversary.

10. Hindu ritual of women being burnt alive on their dead husband's pyre.

11. Provision providing for the offence of statutory rape.

12. Meera Kosambi, 'Girl-Brides and Socio-Legal Change: Age of Consent Bill (1891) Controversy', *Economic and Political Weekly* 26.31/32 (1991). Retrieved from www.jstor.org/stable/41498538 on 9 September 2018.

13. *Queen Empress v. Hari Mohan Maiti* reported as (1890) ILR 18 Cal 49.

14. Donogh, *A Treatise on the Law of Sedition and Cognate Offences in British India.*

15. Ibid.

16. Reported as (1892) ILR 19 Cal 35.

17. *Reg. v. Holbrook & Ors.* reported as L.R. 3 Q.B.D. 60.

18. Mughal Emperor (1618–1707).

19. Muslim general from Bengal who attacked Jagannath Puri in 1568 with his army to tear down the Konark temple.

20. *Reg. v. Sullivan* cited as 11 Cox 45.

21. Present-day Maharashtra.

22. D.V. Athalye, *The Life of Lokamanya Tilak* (Annasahib Chiploonkar, 1921).

23. A political post in native princely states occupied by officers of the British government.

24. *Imperial Gazetteer*, Chapter 10 of Volume III (Oxford Clarendon Press, (1907).

25. Figures for the population affected in princely states were not provided in the *Imperial Gazetteer*.

26. Ajit Kumar Ghose, 'Food Supply and Starvation: A Study of Famines with Reference to the Indian Sub-Continent', *Oxford Economic Papers* 34.2 (1982): 368–89. Retrieved from http://www.jstor.org/stable/2662775 on 9 September 2018.

27. Means 'the Lion'.

28. Anglicization of 'Maratha' which refers to a segment of people from western Maharashtra.

29. The proposals made on 26 October 1890 also included proposals for the prohibition of alcohol, dowry and disfigurement of widows.

30. Athalye, *The Life of Lokamanya Tilak*.

31. Ibid. Tilak resigned from the Legislative Council in 1897 after a prosecution for sedition was initiated against him.

32. *Imperial Gazetteer*, Chapter 10 of Volume III.

33. Athalye, *The Life of Lokamanya Tilak*.

34. Ibid.

35. Ibid.

36. A Muslim general who had attacked Shivaji Maharaj.

37. This term was interpreted by the court to mean a barbarian or foreigner who speaks any language but Sanskrit and is not subject to Hindu institutions. However, other scholars contend that it referred to Muslim invaders and not Christians or other foreigners as interpreted by the Court.

38. The trial of Tilak is reported as (1898) ILR 22 Bombay 112. The report contains the translated text of the speeches and writings for which the prosecution for sedition against Bal Gangadhar Tilak was launched.

39. T.V. Parvate, *Bal Gangadhar Tilak (*Navajivan Publishing House, 1958).

40. N.C. Kelkar, *Full and Authentic Report of the Tilak Trial* (Indu Prakash Press, 1908), republished by the Publications Division of the Ministry of Information and Broadcasting of the Government of India in 2017.

41. T.V. Parvate, *Mahadev Govind Ranade: A Biography* (Asia Publishing House, 1963).

42. Parvate, Supra at footnote 142

43. From the text of the Judgment of the Privy Council in *Gangadhar Tilak v. Queen Empress*, 19 November 1897.

44. Ibid.

45. Parvate, *Bal Gangadhar Tilak*.

46. The district court handling criminal trials is known as the Sessions Court.

47. Donogh, *A Treatise on the Law of Sedition and Cognate Offences in British India*.

48. A newspaper report in *Sydney Morning Herald* dated 25 November 1897 refers to the publication as *Maharani* and the names of the accused as Kishaltar and Harmolkar. The report was retrieved from https://trove.nla.gov.au/newspaper/article/14167690 (accessed 29 September 2018).

49. Translated from the vernacular.

50. *Queen Empress v. Ramchandra Narayan and another,* ILR 22 Bombay 152.

51. Donogh, *A Treatise on the Law of Sedition and Cognate Offences in British India*.

52. Reported as ILR 20 Allahabad 55 (F.B.).

53. Benches comprising of three judges is referred to as a full bench of a High Court.

54. Present-day western Uttar Pradesh.

55. The report of the judgment does not contain the contents of the offending article.

56. Donogh, *A Treatise on the Law of Sedition and Cognate Offences in British India.*
57. Ibid.
58. Ibid.
59. Ibid.
60. Ibid.

Chapter 5: Revolutionary Sedition

1. Lytton Strachey, *Queen Victoria* (Collins, 1958).
2. Arthur Conan Doyle, *The Great Boer War* (George Bell & Sons, 1901).
3. Abraham Ascher, *Russia: A Short History* (Oneworld Publications, 2002).
4. Hirendranath Mukherjee, *India's Struggle for Freedom* (National Book Agency, 1962).
5. Published in Calcutta.
6. Vinod Kumar Saxena, *The Partition of Bengal* (Kanishka Publishing House, 1987).
7. Ibid.
8. 'Hail, Motherland', a poem written by Bankim Chandra Chatterjee in the 1870s and included in his novel *Anandmath.*
9. Saxena, *The Partition of Bengal.*
10. *Bal Gangadhar Tilak: His Writings and Speeches* (Ganesh & Co.)
11. Sukla Sanyal, 'Legitimizing Violence: Seditious Propaganda and Revolutionary Pamphlets in Bengal, 1908–1918', *Journal of Asian Studies* 67.3 (2008). Retrieved from http://www.jstor.org/stable/20203424 on 13 October 2018.
12. Reported as (1908) 35 Cal 945.
13. Donogh, *A Treatise on the Law of Sedition and Cognate Offences in British India.*
14. Ibid.

15.   Sanyal, 'Legitimizing Violence: Seditious Propaganda and Revolutionary Pamphlets in Bengal, 1908–1918'.

16.   In Tamil Nadu.

17.   *Chidambaram Pillai v. Emperor*, reported as ILR 32 Madras 9.

18.   Ibid.

19.   Sitaramayya, *The History of the Indian National Congress (1885–1935)*.

20.   *A Collection of the Acts passed by the Governor General of India in Council 1907* (Calcutta: Superintendent of Government Printing, 1908).

21.   F.C. Daly, *First Rebels: Strictly Confidential Note on the Growth of the Revolutionary Movement in Bengal* (Riddhi India, 1911).

22.   Ibid.

23.   *Sedition Committee Report 1918*, prepared by a committee headed by Justice Sidney Rowlatt.

24.   Ibid.

25.   This chapter relies heavily on the account of the second trial of Tilak contained in *Full & Authentic Report of the Tilak Trial* by N.C. Kelkar (1908), and the judgment of the Bombay High Court as *King Emperor v. Bal Gangadhar Tilak* reported as (1908) 10 BLR 848.

26.   The articles were in the Marathi language. Titles and articles were translated into English for his prosecution.

27.   Leader of the Indian Muslim League and the first governor general of Pakistan.

28.   Kelkar, *Full and Authentic Report of the Tilak Trial*.

29.   Ibid.

30.   Justice Davar was referring to Tilak's previous conviction for sedition and his subsequent release in 1898.

31.   Athalye, *The Life of Lokamanya Tilak*.

32.   Ibid.

33.   Reported as (1910) 12 BOMLR 105.

34. From the abridged English version of *Krantiveer Babarao Savarkar*, a Marathi biography written by D.N. Gokhale (Shrividya Prakashan, 1979). Retrieved from savarkar. org/en/pdfs/babarao-savarkar-v003.pdf (accessed 4 November 2018).

35. Reported as [1910] 12 BOMLR 105.

36. Sedition Committee Report 1918.·

37. Gokhale, *Krantiveer Babarao Savarkar*.

38. As reported by FirstPost on 19 December 2017, https:// www.firstpost.com/politics/lok-sabha-passes-two-bills-to-repeal-245-laws-including-calcutta-pilots-act-prevention-of-seditious-meeting-act-4266527.html.

39. Hirendranath Mukherjee, *India's Struggle for Freedom*.

40. Donogh, *A Treatise on the Law of Sedition and Cognate Offences in British India*.

Chapter 6: Dark Acts and the Black Act

1. Judge of the King's Bench of the High Court of Justice in England.

2. Chief justice of the Bombay High Court.

3. Judge of the Madras High Court.

4. Member of the Board of Revenue of the United Provinces.

5. Lawyer practising in the Calcutta High Court.

6. Resolution No. 2884 dated 10 December 1917 by the home department of the government of India, published along with the Sedition Committee Report in 1918.

7. Covering letter dated 15 April 1918 published along with the Sedition Committee Report in 1918.

8. Chapter 1, 'Revolutionary Conspiracies in Bombay', Sedition Committee Report, 1918.

9. Ibid.

10. Ibid.

11. Ibid.

12. Chapter 4, 'Revolutionary Crime in Bengal', Sedition Committee Report, 1918.
13. Ibid.
14. Prussian general and military historian.
15. Chapter 7, 'German Plots', Sedition Committee Report, 1918.
16. Ibid.
17. Chapter 11, 'Revolutionary Movements in Punjab', Sedition Committee Report, 1918.
18. Ibid.
19. Ibid.
20. Ibid.
21. Present-day Tirunelveli in Tamil Nadu.
22. Chapter 12, 'Revolutionary Crimes in Madras', Sedition Committee Report, 1918.
23. Ibid.
24. Chapter 14, 'A Muhammadan Current', Sedition Committee Report, 1918.
25. Ibid.
26. Chapter 16, 'The Difficulties That Have Arisen in Dealing with the Conspiracies', Sedition Committee Report, 1918.
27. Ibid.
28. Ibid.
29. Chapter 17, 'The Legislation Required', Sedition Committee Report, 1918.
30. Ibid.
31. Ibid.
32. Ibid.
33. Ibid.
34. Ibid.
35. H.N. Mittra, *Punjab Unrest: Before & After,* second edition (Bela Press, 1921).
36. A.G. Noorani, *Indian Political Trials* (Oxford University Press, 2005).

37. Ibid.

38. Judgment dated 9 November 1916 bearing title *Bal Gangadhar Tilak v. Emperor* reported as (1917) 19 BOMLR 211.

39. Judgment reported as (1917) Law Weekly Vol. V Parts 1&2 at Page 1.

40. Ibid.

41. Ibid.

42. Kanji Dwarkadas, *India's Fight for Freedom, 1913–1937: An Eyewitness Story* (New Delhi: Popular Prakashan, 1960).

43. Ibid.

44. Ibid.

45. Statement of Lord Sinha, undersecretary of state for India, to the House of Lords of the British Parliament on 6 August 1919, retrieved from https://hansard.parliament. uk/Lords/1919-08-06/debates/dc781f78-1bdb-4f1d-bcb4-e7ea87273063/MartialLawInIndia (accessed 12 December 2018).

46. Dwarkadas, *India's Fight for Freedom, 1913–1937: An Eyewitness Story*.

47. Ibid.

48. Mittra, *Punjab Unrest: Before & After*.

49. House of Commons Debate, 8 July 1920, Vol. 131 cc1705-819. Retrieved from https://api.parliament.uk/ historic-hansard/commons/1920/jul/08/army-council-and-general-dyer (accessed 12 December 2018).

50. *Bugga v. Emperor,* decided by the Bombay High Court on 20 February 1920 and reported as (1920) 22 BOMLR 609.

51. House of Lords debate on 'Martial Law in India' held on 6 August 1919 (Vol. 36 cc490-504). Retrieved from api.parliament.uk/historic-hansard/lords/1919/aug/06/ martial-law-in-india (accessed 23 December 2018). The debate focused on the treatment meted out to Harkishen Lal by the government of India for which questions were

asked of the British government. Lord Satyendra Prasanna Sinha, the undersecretary of state for India, answered the questions on behalf of the government.

52. *Kali Nath Roy v. King Emperor,* decided by the Bombay High Court on 9 December 1920 and reported as (1921) 23 BOMLR 709.

53. At that time there was no written constitution and litigants relied on the unwritten constitution of the United Kingdom. An unwritten constitution is an uncodified constitution which includes acts of Parliament, judgments of courts and conventions which are customary.

54. *Bugga v. Emperor.*

55. Lord Sinha's address to the House of Lords.

56. Ibid.

Chapter 7: Gandhi, Azad and Nehru: Politics of Sedition

1. Mahatma Gandhi, *Freedom's Battle: A Comprehensive Collection of Writings and Speeches on the Present Situation* (Ganesh & Co., 1922).

2. Ibid.

3. Reliance is placed on *Source Material for a History of the Freedom Movement in India, Vol. III, Parts I–III,* published in 1965 and edited by Prof. N.R. Pathak. These volumes deal specifically with Mahatma Gandhi and cover the period from 1915 up till 1922, the year of his incarceration. The material was collected from the Maharashtra state and government of India records and was published by Government Central Press in Mumbai. A hat-tip to A.G. Noorani whose notes led me to this treasure trove, which consists of many volumes containing authentic information on the Indian independence movement.

4. Mahatma Gandhi's address to a meeting of the *Satyagraha Sabha* in Bombay on 27 April 1919.

5. R.C. Majumdar, *History of the Freedom Movement in India.*

6. Ibid.

7. Ibid.

8. Ibid.

9. Pathak, *Source Material for a History of the Freedom Movement in India, Vol. III, Parts I–III.*

10. Published on 15 June 1921.

11. Published on 29 September 1921.

12. Published on 15 December 1921.

13. Published on 23 February 1922.

14. R.K. Prabhu, *Two Memorable Trials of Mahatma Gandhi* (Navajivan Publishing House, 1962).

15. Ibid.

16. Noorani, *Indian Political Trials.*

17. Mahadev Desai, *Maulana Abul Kalam Azad* (Shiva Lal Agarwala & Co., 1946).

18. Frank Moraes, *Jawaharlal Nehru: A Biography* (Jaico Publishing House, 1959).

19. Retrieved from online resources made available by the Nehru Memorial Museum and Library at http://nehruportal.nic.in/fifth-imprisonment-19-october-1930-26-january-1931 (accessed 19 January 2019).

20. Ibid.

21. Moraes, *Jawaharlal Nehru: A Biography.*

22. *Selected works of Jawaharlal Nehru* (Vol. 6), Jawaharlal Nehru Memorial Fund (1972).

23. Ibid.

24. Nehru's statement to the court contains this contention, Ibid.

25. Nehru's oral statement to the court, Ibid.

26. Ibid.

27. Retrieved from online resources made available by the Nehru Memorial Museum and Library, http://nehruportal.nic.in/

seventh-imprisonment-12-february-1934-%E2%80%93-
3-september-1935 (accessed 19 January 2019).

Chapter 8: No Love Lost

1.   *Kamal Krishna Sircar v. Emperor,* reported as AIR 1935
     Cal 636.
2.   Ibid.
3.   *Satyaranjan Bakshi & anr. v. King Emperor,* reported as
     AIR 1927 Cal 698.
4.   *Vishambar Dayal v. Emperor,* reported as AIR 1941
     Oudh 33.
5.   *Satyaranjan Bakshi & anr. v. King Emperor,* reported as
     AIR 1927 Cal 698.
6.   *In re Anand Bazar Patrika,* AIR 1932 Cal 745.
7.   AIR 1949 Sind 46.
8.   *Kshitij Chandra Roy v. Emperor,* AIR 1932 Cal 547.
9.   Rule 34(6) of the Defence of India Rules 1939.
10. Reported as AIR (29) 1942 FC 22.
11. *Reg. v. Sullivan* cited as 11 Cox 45.
12. Reported in AIR 1947 PC 82.
13. *Queen Empress v. Bal Gangadhar Tilak,* reported in
     (1897) ILR 22.
14. V.P. Menon, *The Transfer of Power in India* (Orient
     Longmans, 1957).
15. Gautam Bhatia, *Offend, Shock or Disturb: Free Speech
     under the Indian Constitution* (Oxford University Press,
     2018).
16. Constitution Assembly Debate dated 29 April 1947.
     Retrieved from cadindia.clpr.org.in/constitution_
     assembly_debates/volume/3/1947-04-29 (accessed 26
     January 2019).
17. Constitution Assembly Debate dated 30 April 1947.
     Retrieved from cadindia.clpr.org.in/constitution_

assembly_debates/volume/3/1947-04-30 (accessed 26 January 2019).

18. Gautam Bhatia, *Offend, Shock or Disturb: Free Speech under the Indian Constitution*.

19. Socialist representative from the United Provinces.

20. Constitution Assembly Debate dated 1 December 1948. Retrieved from cadindia.clpr.org.in/constitution_ assembly_debates/volume/7/1948-12-01 (accessed 26 January 2019).

21. Representative from Bombay.

22. Representative from the Central Provinces.

23. Constitution Assembly Debate dated 1 December 1948. Retrieved from cadindia.clpr.org.in/constitution_ assembly_debates/volume/7/1948-12-02 (accessed 26 January 2019).

Chapter 9: Courting Sedition

1. Reported as AIR (29) 1942 FC 22.

2. Reported in AIR 1947 PC 82.

3. Section 124A underwent cosmetic changes in the years 1937, 1948, 1950, 1951 and 1955. After the amendment of 1955, it has been left untouched by Parliament.

4. Substituted in place of 'transportation for life or any shorter term' in 1955 w.e.f. 1 January 1956.

5. *Tara Singh Gopi Chand v. State*, decided on 28 November 1950, reported as AIR 1951 Punjab 27.

6. Promoting enmity between different groups.

7. Five judges.

8. AIR 1950 SC 124.

9. AIR 1950 SC 129.

10. Extracted in *Ram Nandan v. State*, reported as AIR 1959 All 101.

11. Reported as 1954 CriLJ 758.

12. *Sagolsem Indramani Singh & ors. v. State of Manipur,* reported as 1955 CrLJ 184.

13. *Ram Nandan v. State,* AIR 1959 All 101.

14. Reported as AIR 1962 SC 955.

15. D.R. Mankekar, *The Guilty Men of 1962* (Tulsi Shah Enterprises, 1968).

16. Robert W. Stern, 'The Sino-Indian Border Controversy and the Communist Party of India', *Journal of Politics* 27. 1 (1965). Retrieved from www.jstor.org/stable/2128001 (accessed 29 January 2019).

17. Ibid.

18. Reported as 1967 CriLJ 1110.

19. The Constitution (Sixteenth) Amendment Act, 1963.

20. *Manubhai Tribhovandas Patel v. State of Gujarat & anr.,* reported as 1971 CriLJ 388.

21. Reported as AIR 1976 AP 375.

22. Operation conducted by the Indian military between 1–8 June 1984 to capture and evacuate Jarnail Singh Bhindranwale from Harmandir Saheb, also known as the Golden Temple, the most important shrine for the Sikh community. Bhindranwale was a militant religious leader and the leader of the Khalistani Movement, which demanded secession from the Indian State to form the Sikh state of Khalistan. The operation resulted in the desecration of the shrine and caused major civilian casualties. It actually provided impetus to the Khalistani Movement and was directly responsible for Indira Gandhi's assassination. See 'Operation Blue Star: India's First Tryst with Militant Extremism', *DNA*, 5 November 2016, www.dnai.in/dDSZ (accessed 1 February 2019).

23. *India Today*, 'The Last Day of Indira Gandhi', 31 October 2018, www.indiatoday.in/india/story/the-last-day-of-indira-gandhi-1379440-2018-10-31 (accessed 1 February 2019).

24. *Balwant Singh & anr. v. State of Punjab,* reported as 1995 (1) SCR 411, decided on 1 March 1995.

25. Reported as 1997 (7) SCC 431.

26. *Dr Binayak Sen v. State of Chhattisgarh,* bearing case no. Crl. Appeal 20/2011, decided on 10 February 2011.

27. Ibid.

28. *Binayak Sen v. State of Chhattisgarh,* bearing case no. SLP(Crl) 2053/2011, decided on 15 April 2011.

29. *The Hindu,* 'Binayak Sen Gets Bail in Supreme Court', 15 April 2011, https://www.thehindu.com/news/national/Binayak-Sen-gets-bail-in-Supreme-Court/article14685491.ece (accessed 17 February 2019).

Chapter 10: Stories of Sedition

1. ESPNCricinfo, http://www.espncricinfo.com/series/8532/report/710301/india-vs-pakistan-6th-match-asia-cup-2013-14, 2 March 2014 (accessed 7 February 2019).

2. Published on March 6, 2014 at https://nyti.ms/1ifLxvQ (accessed 7 February 2019).

3. Ibid.

4. *Sanskar Marathe v. State of Maharashtra & ors.,* reported as 2015 CriLJ 3561.

5. Ibid.

6. Writ Petition bearing No. WP(C) 683/2016 titled *Common Cause & anr. v. Union of India.*

7. FIR No. 110/2016 dated 11.02.2016 registered at Vasant Kunj North Police Station, South Delhi District, Delhi

8. District Court for New Delhi District.

9. https://indianexpress.com/article/india/india-news-india/jnu-delhi-police-kanhaiya-kumar-patiala-house-court-india-news (accessed 12 February 2019).

10. Judgment dated March 2, 2016 in WP(Crl) 558/2016 titled *Kanhaiya Kumar v. State of NCT of Delhi.*

11. Ibid.

12. https://www.livelaw.in/news-updates/jnu-sedition-case-delhi-police-files-chargesheet-against-kanhaiya-kumar-umar-khalid-and-others-142103 (accessed 12 February 2019).

13. https://www.livelaw.in/top-stories/setback-to-delhi-police-court-refuses-to-take-cognizance-in-jnu-sedition-case-against-kanhaiya-others-142248 (accessed 12 February 2019).

14. *Salman v. State of Kerala* bearing number B.A. 6811/2014 decided on 22 September 2014.

15. https://www.thenewsminute.com/keralas/316 (accessed 12 February 2019).

16. https://www.thehindu.com/news/national/sc-dismisses-tn-govts-plea-for-police-custody-of-kovan/article7932967.ece (accessed 12 February 2019).

17. https://indianexpress.com/article/india/india-news-india/kudankulam-nuclear-plant-protest-sedition-supreme-court-of-india-section-124a-3024655 (accessed 13 February 2019).

18. Writ Petition bearing No. WP(C) 683/2016 titled *Common Cause & anr. v. Union of India*.

19. http://www.world-nuclear.org/information-library/safety-and-security/safety-of-plants/fukushima-accident.aspx (accessed 13 February 2019).

20. *G. Sundarajan v. Union of India & ors.* bearing case number C.A. 4440 of 2013.

21. https://indianexpress.com/article/india/india-news-india/kudankulam-nuclear-plant-protest-sedition-supreme-court-of-india-section-124a-3024655 (accessed 13 February 2019).

22. https://scroll.in/article/894055/tamil-nadu-has-filed-133-cases-against-this-man-as-part-of-its-crackdown-on-anti-sterlite-protests (14 February 2019).

23. Translates to 'Naked and Hungry India'.

24. Translates to 'Pakistan is dearer than life itself'.

25. From the transcript of Arundhati Roy's speech which was released by her, https://www.dawn.com/news/587809/seditious-speech (accessed 13 February 2019).

26. https://www.telegraph.co.uk/news/worldnews/asia/india/8087820/Arundhati-Roy-could-face-sedition-trial-over-Kashmir-comments.html (accessed 13 February 2019).

27. https://www.theaustralian.com.au/news/world/india-decides-not-to-book-arundhati-roy-with-sedition/news-story/9dd04bec9c06d5e243085c2e41af5e19 (accessed 13 February 2019).

28. *Arun Jaitley v. State of Uttar Pradesh*, Application s/s 482 No. 32703 of 2015, decided on 5 November 2015.

29. Ibid.

30. Translates to 'Long live Pakistan'.

31. https://www.livelaw.in/news-updates/hc-denies-anticipatory-bail-to-whatsapp-group-admin-142437 (accessed 14 February 2019).

32. https://indianexpress.com/article/india/chennai-man-booked-for-sedition-over-message-received-4757129 (accessed 14 February 2019).

33. *Tehseen Poonawala v. Union of India,* bearing number WP(C) 19/2018, decided on 19 April 2018.

34. https://scroll.in/latest/877453/chhattisgarh-journalist-charged-with-sedition-for-sharing-cartoon-on-sc-verdict-in-loya-case (accessed 15 February 2019).

35. https://amp.scroll.in/article/904065/a-journalist-in-manipur-has-been-booked-under-national-security-act-for-facebook-post-against-bjp (accessed 15 February 2019).

36. https://theprint.in/governance/sahitya-akademi-awardee-rti-activist-journalist-charged-with-sedition-for-remarks-on-citizenship-bill/176112 (accessed 15 February 2019).

37. https://indianexpress.com/article/north-east-india/assam/assam-intellectuals-hiren-gohain-akhil-gogoi-

manjit-mahanta-booked-for-sedition-for-remarks-on-citizenship-amendment-bill-5531915/lite/?__twitter_impression=true (accessed 15 February 2019).

38. *Dr Hiren Gohain & ors. v. State of Assam,* bearing case number AB 120/2019.

39. https://thewire.in/government/citizenship-bill-lapses-in-rajya-sabha-what-happens-next (accessed 16 February 2019).

40. *Thokchom Venas v. Commissioner of Police & ors.* bearing number W.P. (Crl.) 530/2019, decided on 18 February 2019.

41. https://indianexpress.com/article/north-east-india/manipur/manipur-charged-with-sedition-student-leader-veewon-thokchom-released-on-bail-5591695 (accessed 31 March 2019).

42. https://timesofindia.indiatimes.com/india/251-sedition-cases-filed-in-assam-since-bjp-came-to-power/articleshow/67830288.cms (accessed 31 March 2019).

43. https://www.hindustantimes.com/india/jharkhand-police-wield-sedition-stick-most-to-hunt-down-maoist-rebels/story-LRjAsNCvstwjtEIS5JJ4LJ.html (accessed 16 February 2019).

44. https://www.newsclick.in/pathalgarhi-movement-massive-crackdown-250-tribals-booked-under-sedition (accessed 16 February 2019).

45. https://www.firstpost.com/india/activists-move-jharkhand-hc-over-fir-alleging-sedition-say-theyre-being-targeted-for-supporting-tribal-rights-5261551.html/amp?__twitter_impression=true (accessed 16 February 2019).

46. *Stan Swamy & ors. v, State of Jharkhand,* bearing case no. Crl. M.P. 3183/2018.

47. J.C. Jha, 'The Tribal Society of Kolhan (Singhbhum) at the Advent of British Rule in 1837–8', *Proceedings of the Indian History Congress* 38 (1977).

48. The state of Bihar was reorganized into the separate states of Bihar and Jharkhand in 2000, with Jharkhand comprising of erstwhile south Bihar which is mineral-rich and has a majority tribal population.

49. https://www.financialexpress.com/india-news/ jharkhand-tribal-group-demands-separate-kolhan-estate-government-43-charged-with-sedition/991411   (accessed 16 February 2019).

Chapter 11: The Road Ahead

1. https://www.indiatoday.in/india/story/exclusive-mha-data-shows-only-2-convicted-under-sedition-law-in-3-years-1289231-2018-07-18 (accessed 16 February 2019).

2. The 42nd report of the Law Commission of India.

3. https://www.pressgazette.co.uk/criminal-libel-and-sedition-offences-abolished (accessed 17 February 2019).

4. Rajya Sabha supplement to synopsis of debate, 9 August 2019.

5. Ibid.

Index